# *STAYING UP WHEN YOUR JOB PULLS YOU DOWN*

# STAYING UP WHEN YOUR JOB PULLS YOU DOWN

Joanne Bodner and
Venda Raye-Johnson

A PERIGEE BOOK

Perigee Books
are published by
The Putnam Publishing Group
200 Madison Avenue
New York, NY 10016

Library of Congress Cataloging-in-Publication Data
Bodner, Joanne, date
Staying up when your job pulls you down / Joanne Bodner
and Venda Raye-Johnson.
p.     cm.
ISBN 0-399-51673-5
1. Job satisfaction.   2. Occupational mobility.   3. Career
development.   I. Raye-Johnson, Venda, date.   II. Title.
HF5549.5.J63B63   1991              90-26959   CIP
650.1—dc20

Printed in the United States of America

4   5   6   7   8   9   10

*This book is dedicated to the following people:*

To my husband, Drew, and to my parents,
Herbert and Lucille Records.
JOANNE BODNER

To my husband, Bill, and my Father.
VENDA RAYE-JOHNSON

# Contents

# STAYING UP WHEN YOUR JOB PULLS YOU DOWN

# INTRODUCTION

"I'VE BEEN THE manager of our direct-mail operations for eight years now. I make good money and I like my work, but there are so many problems. I think it's time for me to move on." Stephanie shrugged her shoulders, punctuating her resolution to change jobs. She had been extremely frustrated and unhappy for several years now and finally decided to do something about it. So she came to us for help in her job search.

"Really, what I'm best at is training new company presidents!" Stephanie said with a grimace. "I'm working on my third one now. In the meantime I've had nearly the same responsibilities for years, and all I seem to do is put out fires. It doesn't seem like I'm accomplishing anything."

With these words, the floodgates opened and Stephanie seemed to let all her pent-up frustrations spill out. "Another thing that upsets me is that my boss gives me projects to do and then doesn't give me any directions on how to do them. Right now I've been told to develop a marketing program—but I'm just hanging there with no direction, spinning my wheels."

We began to further explore the job problem with Stephanie. She continued. "When I do speak out and ask for help," she insisted, "my boss always says something to placate me for a while. I think I want to work for a company that has a lot more structure—someplace where I'll know what's expected of me."

Stephanie had been submerged in a pool of job problems for some time now and was treading water to keep from going under. And, she is not alone! It has been estimated that more than twenty million American workers are in the same boat. They are unhappy with their jobs and are trying to stay afloat, just like Stephanie.

This sense of "going nowhere" leads to absenteeism, job burnout, low productivity, and above all, job changing. The 1989 book *Work in the New Economy*, copublished by the American Association of Counseling and Development, makes the startling statement that "almost 30% of all American workers have been with their present employer for one year or less." Job changing in America has been described as playing musical chairs.

But while many people are playing musical chairs, there are more and more people who have many good reasons to consider staying where they are and making their jobs work for them. You may be one of them.

More than ever, American workers have entered an era in which there will be solid reasons for staying on the job, despite the problems. The positives outweigh the negatives. Family responsibilities will make us more concerned about job and fringe benefits such as health and child care. Retirement benefits and profit sharing will be looked at more closely. Rapid technical and social changes will make us long for some amount of stability—especially in our job.

From our twenty-plus years of career counseling and conducting career training, we know that a large portion of this job-changing behavior stems from feeling pulled down on our job. That pulling-down feeling is one of helplessness, frustration, anger, and apathy. Our clients come to us like Stephanie—as if they were barely staying up. When they feel like they're about to go under, they do the best thing they know how to do—change jobs!

Before long, however, many of them are being pulled down again. The problems they left behind begin to surface again. And so the job-changing cycle stays in effect, creating a sense of futility and frustration for workers and costing employers millions of dollars.

Are you treading water too? Do job problems have you about to go under? Take this self-inventory to find out. Do you:

\_\_\_\_\_ Dread the thought of getting up in the morning?

\_\_\_\_\_ Go to work angry and depressed?

\_\_\_\_\_ Lack a sense of meaning and purpose about your job?

\_\_\_\_\_ Lack a sense of accomplishment on your job?

\_\_\_\_\_ Long for greater control over job situations?

\_\_\_\_\_ Believe you are a peon with little say-so?

\_\_\_\_\_ Feel fed up with co-workers?

\_\_\_\_\_ Frequently come to work late, leave early, or call in sick?

\_\_\_\_\_ Believe your boss is too difficult to work for?

\_\_\_\_\_ Lack enthusiasm in your work?

\_\_\_\_\_ Think that enjoying your work is impossible?

\_\_\_\_\_ Feel like Rodney Dangerfield—"don't get no respect"?

If you checked any of these statements, you may be experiencing "pulling-down times" as your job begins to take control, leaving you feeling helpless and over-whelmed. It becomes difficult to remember the pluses of the job because the minuses are grabbing for your full attention. Like Stephanie, you might be about to jump into another job without thinking through the real issues of your job frustrations. Here are questions to consider first:

1. Am I clear on what the real conflict issues are on my job?
2. Do I understand the big picture of my organization and the changes which are taking place in it?
3. Have I examined my attitudes about a job and are they realistic?
4. Am I clear on my definition of work and what it should provide me?

5. Have I established a sense of purpose and direction in my life?
6. Do I accept who I am as a person?
7. Do I compare myself with others too much?
8. Have I tried developing plans and strategies to work through the job conflict?
9. Have I creatively sought opportunities to fulfill my needs and to express who I am on the job?
10. Have I looked for ways to help others express who they are on the job?

Stephanie wanted to change jobs before she had explored the deeper issues. She focused on her job problems so much that she overlooked many of the merits of her job. She made a good salary, the company had great benefits, and she felt relatively secure in her job. It was the nagging feeling of always putting out fires and going nowhere that kept Stephanie feeling as if she were treading water.

How do we deal with job frustrations, disappointments, and the daily grind more effectively—without changing jobs? How do we stop treading water and begin to swim instead?

We believe job satisfaction hinges on three simple principles:

1. Each one of us must be responsible for our individual definition of job satisfaction.
2. Once we have clarified what we really want from

15

our job, we must reframe our thinking about our relationship to it.

3. When we reframe our thinking, we must take action to magnify the positive parts of our job and to minimize the negative ones. By concentrating on the portions of our job that we find enjoyable, or at least tolerable, we can begin to maximize and maintain that enjoyment by generating more positive feelings and opportunities for ourselves.

*Staying Up When Your Job Pulls You Down* can help you prepare to do this. The underlying philosophy of this book is that the only real control we have in this constantly changing world is over ourselves. We can't always change circumstances, but we can reframe our thinking to bring out the best in the situation. In other words we can still make lemonade out of lemons! We can learn problem-solving skills that empower us to be the managers of our own lives.

*Staying Up When Your Job Pulls You Down* is a how-to book that will teach you steps and skills to further your job satisfaction. You will practice choosing what we term "staying-up behaviors" that will create positive personal change. Specifically, you will learn how to get a firmer understanding of yourself and your motivations, determine what you really want from a job, and use job problems for self-development.

We have devised a strategy that will help you do this in a systematic fashion. We call this the ADD Strategy. The ADD Strategy is a simple method designed to:

_____ Analyze the problem and its root source

_____ Determine what you really want from your job

_____ Develop an action plan to use staying-up behaviors that will help you get what you really want

It has been used successfully with hundreds of our clients, and we believe it can work for you, too. So if you feel like you are treading water and are about to go under—hold on. We think we have a lifesaver; it's called *Staying Up When Your Job Pulls You Down*.

# CHAPTER 1

## Who Are You—Really?

ALL OF US have heard of people who got fed up with their jobs, quit on Monday morning, and landed a much better-paying job by that Friday—as if by fate! We have read about the manager who was passed over for a long-awaited promotion and who wasted little time in generating a job offer to become the chief executive officer for a leading competitor. It sounds so simple!

But let's face the truth. Such examples are pipe dreams for many of us. These people are the exceptions, not the rule. Top-level managers may be able to move from company to company, building up benefits and perks as they go. But average midmanagers or office workers rarely have such "movability." In fact, few of us are positioned well enough to demand or to negotiate such favorable results.

Even worse, many American workers have been caught in a squeeze between the sometimes conflicting trends of today's workplace. Corporate takeovers, flatten-ing organizations, and downsizings abound at alarming rates, making many workers fearful that they might be next in the pink-slip line. And this fear may be well grounded. According to some estimates, more than twenty-five million workers will be unemployed at some time in their working career. These corporate layoffs are occurring at a time when job security and the resulting financial stability have become a high priority for many people.

Dual-career couples have become dependent on two incomes just to maintain their standard of living. Single parents struggle to meet child care and commuting costs without a second income to fall back on in an emergency. Many workers in both categories encounter a newer American dilemma—responsibility for aging parents as well as for children.

And in the midst of these problems is the fact that many of today's workers will encounter significant bar-riers to career advancement. The traditional route to higher salaries and career prestige has required people to climb the corporate ladder. This has meant paying dues in middle-management positions. Yet, with the "lean and mean" philosophies that organizations are moving to-ward, many of these midmanagement positions are being eliminated, thus removing a once taken-for-granted stepping-stone into top management.

Baby boomers, particularly, will continue to vie with the myriad of other talented workers for those fewer middle-management spots in corporations. Most American workers fall into this category. Now between 25 and 45 years old, many of them are approaching middle age and have plateaued in their career advancement. They are becoming disillusioned about making it to the top.

Mike, a 34-year-old client of ours, went to work right out of college as an assistant manager for a Fortune 500 tire manufacturer and retailer. He set a goal for himself right away. He wanted to become a regional manager.

Almost ten years have passed, and Mike has yet to be promoted to regional manager. For the first seven years, the company grew and Mike grew right along with it. He was transferred to larger stores, his stores always met their quotas, and he polished his management skills.

Three years ago, however, the corporation ran into a retail slump. Several hundred workers were laid off, five stores were closed, and Mike's career goals were put on hold. Mike was encouraged to be patient and hold tight. The market would change, Mike's boss said, and when it did, Mike would be the one sent to head up the region he had his eye set on.

"But what am I waiting for?" Mike asked us. "How do I know they really mean it? It's been almost three years now, and I haven't even gotten a raise. I'm bailing out." Mike had come to believe he would be better off going to another company. He was disappointed and frustrated. And, above all, he was starting to get depressed. He had decided to begin sending out résumés.

What were Mike's chances, though, with another company? How did he know that the same thing wouldn't happen all over again? What if he changed jobs and found himself faced with a similar set of problems? Would he have gained anything?

As it turned out, Mike was startled at the results of his preliminary job search. After sending résumés to about twenty-five companies, he received only three inter-views. Two were for store manager positions and one was for outside sales. In addition, he found that these com-panies' growth potential looked no brighter than the growth of his present company.

For the first time Mike really understood exactly what had been happening in his industry. As companies streamlined to meet budgets, they had cut a layer of middle management. And without that layer, fewer peo-ple had the chance to get the training or exposure to advance into top management. He realized he was posi-tioned better to become a regional manager right where he was after all.

Other employees are finding themselves plateaued in their work, as Mike did. Few will actually make it to the top. Some may even find themselves several rungs lower on the career ladder due to mergers, buyouts, and corporate-wide downsizings. Others will continue in their current midmanagement positions until they retire.

Like Mike, many will decide to change jobs. Encour-aged by self-help books on the fantastic rewards of risk-taking, they will attempt a freedom leap to new positions that promise better futures. Some will be trying to find an empty rung on the career ladder that will increase their paychecks while shortening the climb to the top. Others will hope to discover career satisfaction.

American workers change jobs on the average of every 2½ years. Unfortunately, many times it is jumping from the proverbial frying pan into the fire. After only a few weeks or months, the same job frustrations begin to surface again. Instead of opportunities for advancement, people find themselves last in the line of competent contenders for the decreasing number of management slots. Workloads expand while paychecks stay the same. Family responsibilities intensify as fast as the cost of living increases.

Had Mike taken a job as a department manager with another company, he would have found himself an unknown newcomer to a new boss and to the other department managers. He would have sacrificed whatever seniority he has now. Also, he might have found that his workload had increased over his current job.

In short, while some of us can play the job-hopping game to fame and fortune, most of us will have to endure the increasing frustrations that are occurring in the workplace. The fact is that many of us have good reasons for staying with our current employer, despite the drawbacks present on our job. Insurance benefits, job accessibility, and vestment programs become golden handcuffs for many of us.

The truth is that the stability of our current job can be a comfort for many of us who find ourselves in the midst of rapid changes in other facets of our lives. For the first time in history we are living in several ages at once—the information, space, communications, and high-technology ages—all of which present us with changes daily. Often, the last thing we need to face is learning a new work environment, too.

Just the same, dissatisfaction with job conditions, not to mention the stress of relationships with bosses and co-workers, can leave us feeling out-of-control, lethargic, and helpless. So, with gritted teeth and layers of defensiveness, we learn to deal with the job frustrations by acquiring a tunnel vision that is focused on the future date of our retirement—or job change. We become on-the-job prisoners—powerless victims trapped within our own work environment. The risks of leaving the job may be too high, and yet staying also is a miserable thought.

Sometimes workers develop undesirable methods of coping with job dissatisfaction—such as overeating, overdrinking, or oversleeping. Some become chronic gripers, poisoning co-workers with anger and bitterness. Yet others go through the motions of working. Still others hole up in their office or at their desk, coping with the pain by burying themselves in their work.

We believe that individuals can learn the skills to re-frame their view of the situation rather than focusing on the problem itself. If we were to compare ourselves to two people looking at a glass of water, we need to be like the person who sees the glass as being half full—not the person who sees the same glass as being half empty. By managing our point of view, we open ourselves to a smorgasbord of choices for meeting our own needs and creating our own job satisfaction right where we are—in the job we have now.

Stephanie, our example in the introduction, needed to

get a new angle on what was happening in her job. Unlike Mike, Stephanie was not interested in getting into a higher-level position. She merely wished her boss would stop giving her large projects without direction.

To Stephanie, when the responsibility for a project was delegated to her, she expected also to be told the outcome. Because her boss did not spell out his expectations, it is possible he was complimenting her for having good problem-solving skills. But Stephanie interpreted this action as taking her for granted.

Stephanie's attention had become focused entirely on the problem at hand. She did not stop to consider that her understanding of responsibility might be different from her boss's. Had she reframed her point of view of the situation instead of concentrating on her frustration, she might have been able to solve her own problem.

How can we begin seeing the glass as half full? How can we reframe our viewing point? We must embark on a journey to the center of our very being.

The first stage in this journey to job satisfaction is stepping back and looking directly at *who we are* and *what we really want*. This is not always easy because it means asking ourselves difficult, sometimes painful questions, such as:

· Who am I?
· Do I really like who I am?
· Do I like who I'm turning out to be?
· How can I become the person I want to be?

Yet these philosophical and somewhat transcendent questions need to be confronted if we are to be honest with ourselves about what we want from life and how we can find it through our work.

As career counselors, we have worked with hundreds of clients who have experienced frustration, job dissatisfaction, and depression stemming from their jobs. From our observations and counseling, we have come to several conclusions.

1. The real cause of the person's unhappiness often is hidden—cloaked under such comments as "There's no room for advancement," "My boss won't help me get ahead," or "My job just isn't paying enough."

2. There is a common theme among the stories we hear—it is an underlying negative self-concept that reflects feelings of helplessness, anger, and despair.

3. Because of this negative self-concept, the person has begun to act with self-defeating—and sometimes self-destructive—behaviors that perpetuate the problem.

An example is a man who came to one of our career workshops. Fred enrolled in the workshop because he wanted to change jobs. As the group took turns sharing their reasons for taking the workshop, Fred spoke about his situation. "I started with my company two years ago and felt like I was their rising star. My boss and I got along great—I was his right-hand man. We really were a great team. Then the bomb fell."

Fred grimaced and went on to tell how he had been in line for a promotion but the position was given to someone else. Fred's pain was reflected in his facial expressions and his sarcastic tone of voice. If he could not mask his bitterness among those of us at the workshop, we could only guess that it was even worse at work.

Fred could not see that he was turning this situation into a personal failure. He no longer believed his company saw him as being a valuable employee. His self-concept had changed from being a person in control of his career to one of a helpless victim. As a result Fred was contemplating a job change that may have been premature. Everything else about his current position still attracted him. He liked the work as well as his co-workers, and the company was making a profit.

What if Fred had been able to recognize that he was the same competent person, even though he had faced a setback? It was only his own self-concept that had been changed. What if he could have looked within himself for encouragement instead of feeling his happiness was his company's responsibility?

Perhaps he still would have decided to make a job change, but his positive self-concept would have remained intact. The change then would have been his own decision, not the result of his company's actions.

Mike, our earlier example, also developed a negative self-concept when he was not promoted. He related a story similar to Fred's. "They promoted this other guy, and was he dumb! I mean, I had this idea to develop new services for our key clients. It really worked. We got several new accounts from it—and national ones at that! Then they promoted that bozo and told me they can't even give me a raise! Give me a break!"

While we can't be sure why the "bozo" got a promotion and Mike didn't, we do know that Mike's self-concept was affected as a result. It no longer mattered that his boss was giving him a logical explanation—the company was having hard times, but Mike would be considered for advancement as soon as the company revived. Instead, Mike began to seethe with resentment and to doubt himself.

## THE SELF-CONCEPT AND HOW IT DEVELOPS

What exactly is a self-concept? Why is it so important in our lives? How can a negative self-concept make us unhappy enough to consider leaving the security of our job, as Fred and Mike did?

Our self-concept is the image or picture we have of ourselves. It is our individuality, the special factors that distinguish us from other people.

This self-concept begins from the time we are born. When we are babies and toddlers, our entire attention is focused on ourselves.

As we continue through childhood, we gradually become aware that other people are separate from ourselves.

From the moment we discover that we have a self, we are preoccupied with learning what that "self" is and how to express it. It becomes the age-old question, "Who am I?"

Our self-concept is influenced by internal and external messages. Each time we interact with another person or have an experience, we get messages which we internalize. We draw conclusions from these messages. These messages validate or conflict with the view we have of ourselves. We draw conclusions about what we like or don't like, what is important to us, and what we're good at. Like a photo collage, each of these snapshots becomes a part of the composite picture we have of ourselves.

Each time we add a view to our self-concept from an experience we've had, we also make a judgment as to whether we like the picture we have of ourselves at that moment. If we're satisfied with what we see, our self-concept will be positive. If the message denies us the basic ingredients of a positive self-concept, we might develop a negative concept of ourselves instead.

These basic ingredients are Respect, Responsibility, and Recognition. We call them the Basic Three Rs. As we continue in the book, we will explore these basics in more detail. For right now, let's explore your self-concept.

Take a minute to complete the following self-concept assessment to see how positive your self-concept is right now.

## HOW POSITIVE IS YOUR SELF-CONCEPT?

Answer the following statements as truthfully as possible. Next to each statement put the number that best describes how much you agree with the statement.

4 = Always agree
3 = Almost always agree
2 = Sometimes agree
1 − Almost never agree
0 = Never agree

_____ 1. I'm a cheerful person.

_____ 2. People usually like me.

_____ 3. I have energy and enthusiasm.

_____ 4. If I had a chance, I don't think I would trade places with anyone.

_____ 5. I don't feel ashamed about many things.

_____ 6. I feel that I am unique.

_____ 7. My physical appearance is okay with me.

_____ 8. I have a basically optimistic outlook.

_____ 9. I deserve the good things that have happened to me.

_____10. My personal relationships are satisfying.

_____11. I usually get along with my co-workers.

_____12. I can carry on a conversation with most people.

_____13. I usually don't say things I don't mean.

_____14. I'd like to have a friend like me.

_____15. I don't blow my mistakes up into something they really aren't.

Now add up your score: _____. Here is what it means:

54 or above    You have a very positive self-concept.

38-53          You seem to have a fairly positive self-concept.

22-37          You may have some mixed views of yourself, some positive and some negative.

21 or below    You're not feeling positive about yourself. Perhaps you are just feeling low right now. If your feelings are always like this, you could have a negative self-concept.

If at this time your self-concept is not very positive, perhaps you are allowing your view of your job to influence how you see yourself. When people have frustrating and unhappy experiences at work, they sometimes come to view themselves in a negative light. And it's only natural to want to run away from experiences that make us feel badly about ourselves. In order to take control of the situation and change your view, let's look further at how your job and your self-concept are intertwined.

# CHAPTER 2

## Our Job—
## Our Self-Concept

WHAT DOES OUR job have to do with our self-concept? Why is a positive self-concept so important in job satisfaction?

We spend more than 75 percent of our adult lives working; thus, about 75 percent of our self-concept as adults is formed from the experiences we have on the job. Nowhere else do we learn so much about our skills and our talents, as well as our limitations, as we do on our job.

Work is such an important seasoning in our self-concept. In fact, studies report that people would continue working even if they had won several million dollars. Our self-concept becomes so wrapped up in our job that we no longer work for just the paycheck. Rather, we allow our job to influence our sense of identity.

As counselors, we have had clients whose job experiences did not match the view they had of themselves, and who became unhappy in their job. Through counseling they were able to break the cycle by changing that viewpoint and, thus, the way they were reacting. They regained their positive self-concept. In other words they became their "old selves" again.

Nancy was a client who came to us for help in preparing her résumé for a career change. She came for her appointment ready to do battle with anyone in her way. She stormed into the office complaining about the lack of parking spaces and demanded the secretary let us know right away that she was there.

When we began going over Nancy's résumé, she impatiently nagged, "Just tell me what I need to say. That's what I came here for. I don't know why we have to talk about it so much." We had to spend at least thirty minutes convincing Nancy that we couldn't know what to put on her résumé unless she told us about her current position and her accomplishments!

"I'm a grade school principal," Nancy started. "I've been a principal for five years now. But if I'm going to be a manager, I might as well go into business where my management skills will make some money and have some prestige. No one really takes school people very seriously."

Nancy rattled these statements off as if they were a prepared speech. She spoke in a monotone voice that gave the impression she had memorized her lines. When we asked her to elaborate on a few points, she continued her speech as if on cue.

"If I don't get out now, I never will. Right now it's possible that a company will see that I have skills that can transfer to another field. If I stay in education very much longer, though, there is no company that will take a chance on me. Everyone knows that most educators can't really cut it in competitive enterprise."

As Nancy relaxed a little, she began talking about her education and her first job. She had gone to college to become a teacher—much to the dismay of her mother, who had been a sixth-grade teacher for almost forty years. Nancy's mother had done everything she could to talk Nancy out of her career choice.

During the past five years she had been a school principal, Nancy had come to the conclusion that everything her mother said was true. People really didn't treat teachers the way they used to. The problems with discipline really were getting worse. The money really didn't make all the problems seem worthwhile.

Nancy liked the people she worked with and she was extremely popular with the teachers in the school. She had been successful in solving some of the problems the teachers had struggled with under other principals, but she kept feeling as though she should be doing more— that she needed new challenges.

Yet the only place in management she could move was to a district administrator, and that brought back all the messages she had heard from her mother over the years about school personnel. She finally decided to take the big step and change into a different field while she still had time. What had started as a routine résumé preparation had turned into a full-blown counseling session!

Nancy had been listening to her mother and became very confused about her own self-concept. She thought perhaps she had become a teacher and a principal just to spite her mother. Now she decided to take her mother's advice and become a business executive. She no longer believed in the view she had of herself. And her actions were shouting loud and clear that something was wrong!

When Nancy reviewed all of the reasons she went into teaching in the first place, she discovered she had several good ones. Part of it, of course, was that she admired her mother and genuinely wanted to become a teacher like her. Beyond this, she valued education and felt this was one way in which she could make a lasting contribution to society.

And yet Nancy had to admit her real talents seemed to lie in doing administrative work. While she loved being in the classroom, she found particular pleasure in her ability to bring teachers, parents, and school administrators together to resolve issues. This view of herself matched some of the qualities her mother saw in her. Nancy was a natural leader—she had the initiative, as well as the social skills, to interact with a variety of people. Also, she was an excellent problem solver.

Finally Nancy came to the conclusion that becoming a business executive would be matching her mother's view of her rather than her own self-concept. Instead, being a school administrator was a very close match with the picture she had of herself—the picture that had developed from all of her life experiences. Once she got her positive self-concept back, Nancy's attitude changed and her job dissatisfaction disappeared. She left counseling with the career goal of remaining in the field of education and becoming a superintendent one day.

## What Do People Want?

In *What Do People Want?*, a study by the 1983 Public Agenda Foundation, ten top factors were identified concerning what employees wanted from their work. They were:

1. Work for an efficient manager
2. Think for oneself
3. See end result of one's work
4. Be assigned interesting work
5. Be kept informed
6. Be listened to
7. Be respected
8. Be recognized for one's efforts
9. Be challenged
10. Have opportunities for skill development

This study confirms our experiences in counseling students, housewives, managers, professionals, and clerical and trade personnel. We have three strong statements that summarize our beliefs:

_____ First, we believe that the main ingredients to a positive self-concept are a strong sense of Respect, Responsibility, and Recognition within ourselves. These are basic esteem ingredients we refer to as the Basic Three Rs. They positively feed the self-concept.

_____ Second, when we have a positive attitude about ourselves, we will have a more positive attitude about work, even during times when our job pulls us down.

_____ Third, when we experience a positive view of ourselves and our work, we begin to adopt positive behaviors that can help us stay up during those pulling-down times.

The Three Rs are the basic ingredients to a positive self-concept that leads to job satisfaction. While rewards such as salary raises, promotions, and impressive titles can make our job much more attractive, these rewards are not enough. Job satisfaction occurs only when inner needs for Respect, Responsibility, and Recognition also are met.

## THE ADD STRATEGY

To add more of the Basic Three Rs to our self-concept, we need to reframe the way we view ourselves. Then we can take positive control of our responses and create our own job satisfaction.

To help you begin to analyze your hidden needs and motives, to determine what you really want, and to gain control over yourself, we have developed the ADD Strategy. Using the ADD's systematic method of working through your job problems, you will structure your work environment to meet your basic needs for more Respect, Responsibility, and Recognition. You will learn to select productive behaviors instead of counterproductive ones. The productive behaviors ultimately will increase your Basic Three Rs, which in turn will help you maintain a positive self-concept and to stay up during trying situations.

How does the ADD Strategy work? Let's look at the strategy.

A = Analyze your behaviors. Good mentors have long known that the first step in changing their students' behavior is to analyze what they currently are doing. We cannot know which behaviors need to be changed or how to go about changing them unless we first know exactly *what is happening* and *how it affects us.*

D = Determine what it is you really want. Which aspects of the Basic Three Rs is your self-concept lacking? Do you feel respected? Are you trusted with important tasks? Do people really recognize your good work? Or maybe you are in a situation where you need to add more of all three Rs to your self-concept.

D = Develop an action plan to get what you really want. During this stage you will replace any counterproductive behaviors with productive ones and develop action steps. This in turn will help you attain any or all of the Basic Three Rs— that is, what you really want. Too many good intentions fail because we do not have a specific plan to change. By carefully creating one, we can successfully develop new, productive behaviors that will give us back our positive self-concept.

Another client of ours, Carolyn, was an administrative assistant in an up-and-coming computer-manufacturing firm. In the four years she had worked for the company, she had learned several new software programs, handled all the department's orders, and organized the activities of all the salespersons. Carolyn was ambitious and wanted to progress to a higher position in the company. She came for career counseling because she felt she had been dead-ended by her boss.

"He keeps me away from anything that could help me get promoted," Carolyn explained. "I have a lot of ideas that he thinks are really good, but he won't let me go to meetings to present them. He goes himself. In fact, a couple of times I've heard about one of my ideas later— only by then everyone thinks it's *his* idea!"

Carolyn went on. "I've always told him I'd like to have my own department someday. And he really encourages me! He gives me the highest ratings on my evaluations, and he's gotten me several steep raises. But he's never said anything about helping me when I've talked about my future."

Carolyn's problem was a very subtle one. Her boss

obviously depended on her and valued her work. Carolyn, in turn, had learned a great deal from this person and was loyal to him. Yet she was being taken advantage of and it was starting to show up in the view she had of herself—her self-concept.

Carolyn was not having her Basic Three-R needs met. She felt that if her boss really respected her, he would allow her to attend meetings. If she indeed had any responsibility, she would be able to sign her own name to memos and letters. And if she was really doing a good job, by now he would have helped her be recognized with a promotion.

Carolyn appreciated all other aspects of her work and really did not want to leave her job or the company. She saw no way, however, of advancing as long as she reported to this particular boss. All of this led to such feelings of resentment that it sapped Carolyn's energy level and her motivation. She even became irritable with the few people who reported to her and spent a great deal of time sulking in her office.

Using the ADD Strategy, Carolyn was able to determine her Basic Three-R needs, change her behaviors, and restore her positive self-concept. When she viewed herself as a respected person with responsibility, who was recognized for her achievements, she regained her job satisfaction. How did it work?

The ADD Strategy's emphasis on productive, or staying-up, behaviors made it possible for Carolyn to change her self-concept.

In the next few chapters we will look more closely at

the specifics of how Carolyn, as well as others, used the three steps of the ADD Strategy. We will examine different ways of reacting to problem situations, explore the concepts of Respect, Responsibility, and Recognition, and practice developing action plans. And, we will learn how to ADD the Basic Three Rs to our self-concept to equal job satisfaction!

# CHAPTER 3

## Step One:
## Analyze Your
## Behaviors

THE PURPOSE OF the ADD Strategy is to develop a plan for staying up when our job pulls us down. This requires us to take an honest look at our own behaviors when we find ourselves dissatisfied with our job. Since we cannot always change the situation, and since we cannot change other people, we need to focus on the only thing we can control—ourselves.

When work situations pull us down, we sometimes react with behaviors that express our needs but do little to get the need met. These behaviors are actually counter-productive to addressing the need.

### What Is Behavior?

This is a question that has no simple answer, and that in fact is the subject of several complicated psychological theories. Quite simply put, a behavior is the outward expression of our attitudes.

Others cannot see the thoughts, feelings, and beliefs that go into our attitudes, however. Instead, they observe only our behaviors. Consider these scenarios that are repeated daily in offices across the country.

SCENE: Dennis is passed over for a promotion.
THOUGHT: They think I'm not capable. I'm not respected; I'm not being recognized.
FEELING: I'm really hurt that they picked someone else.
BELIEF: I'll never get ahead.
BEHAVIOR: I'm not even going to try anymore.

Or how about this story?

SCENE: Andrea is assigned a routine project.
THOUGHT: Oh, no! Not that stupid project again! They think I'm not capable of doing anything else.
FEELING: I'm really humiliated that they don't give me more important things to do.
BELIEF: I'm just a flunky.
BEHAVIOR: I'll put it off as long as I can.

All we see as observers is the person's outward behavior. We do not know the thoughts or feelings that led to the behavior. Instead we see only that Dennis is apathetic and that Andrea procrastinates.

Both of these scenes describe stressful, pulling-down situations that trigger behaviors that try to help the person cope with disappointment, anger, and hurt. Neither of these behaviors, however, works to resolve the problem or improves the person's image. Instead, others might view these people as being uncooperative or negative, and they might even begin to view themselves that way.

## From the Playground to the Workground

How do we learn this way of responding? Where do these ineffective coping behaviors begin? As children, we often must act one way when we feel another way. For example, when children feel overpowered by those who are bigger than they are, they know they cannot control what is really wrong, and so they express their frustrations through acting-out behaviors. Some children bully other children, some pout, and others retreat into a fantasy world.

As adults, we are not much different. Just as children act out their frustrations, so adults often have their own variations of acting-out. Perhaps they become aggressive, starting arguments or confronting others. Or perhaps they withdraw, become passive, quiet, sullen, even openly critical. Take office cynics for example. They may be persons who have been passed over for promotions on several occasions. They long for recognition and appreciation. As an expression of this need, their bullying may now come in the form of verbal attacks, usually directed toward those persons felt to be denying them their need for recognition.

These responses are acting-out behaviors, not so far removed from our childhood. They express our job frustrations, but they do not resolve the problem, and they certainly do not allow us to feel good about ourselves.

We need to learn to respond to pulling-down situations with staying-up behaviors. Instead of acting out our frustrations, staying-up behaviors work to resolve the problem, and they allow us to feel good about ourselves.

### Using the ADD Strategy to Analyze Our Behaviors

In step one of the ADD Strategy, Analyze Your Behaviors, we will do three things. First, we will assess our reactions to specific pulling-down situations and begin to identify our acting-out behaviors. Second, we will use other people's observations to help us identify our acting-out behaviors. And third, we will explore our childhood memories for a new understanding of our behaviors. All this will set the stage for adopting new, staying-up behaviors in the future.

## BEHAVIOR SELF-ASSESSMENT

All of us tend to resort to acting-out behaviors when pulling-down situations make us feel out-of-control. These behaviors are familiar and they help us to cope for the time being. After a while, however, a behavior pattern develops that might be comfortable but that is ineffective.

For example, one client we worked with, Aaron, told us that he was burned out from having so much work to complete. To make the matter worse, several of Aaron's co-workers were able to finish their own work and leave right at quitting time, while Aaron often stayed late at the office.

When he did an assessment of his behaviors, Aaron finally concluded that because he did not assert himself by speaking with his supervisor about his workload, he was given more and more work to do. As a result, Aaron wound up with more than his share of work as well as a great deal of resentment. Additionally, he discovered that this same pattern had occurred in the past on other jobs.

**Your Turn**

First assess your behaviors using the following questions to find out how you might be acting out your job problems. Check the most appropriate answer that reflects how you react to the situation described.

1. When a co-worker criticizes your work, you have a tendency to

_____ a. Get angry and blow up when you've "heard enough."

_____ b. Withdraw, cry, or pout.

45

_____ c. Ignore the remark.

_____ d. Deny you heard it or get away quickly from the person who said it.

_____ e. Diplomatically ask the person to explain such a statement.

2. If someone else gets the promotion you thought you earned, you

_____ a. File a grievance against the interviewer.

_____ b. Lose all enthusiasm for any of your work.

_____ c. Begin pulling out all your documentation to explain why you were the best choice.

_____ d. Begin preparing yourself for the next opportunity in your company.

3. When your anger and frustration with your boss begins mounting, you

_____ a. Begin smirking at the "ridiculous" requests she asks of you.

_____ b. Punk your hair as a means of protesting.

_____ c. Get "ill" before an important meeting or project.

_____ d. Calmly but assertively ask your boss to have a private meeting to discuss your concerns.

4. When your job is no longer challenging and you

are doing humdrum, routine work day in and day out, you

_____ a. Lose interest in your work and begin to do just enough to get by.

_____ b. Do nothing and hope you get fired.

_____ c. Don't do your work and find excuses why you didn't get it done.

_____ d. Find creative ways of doing your same job so as to downplay the tedium and still have fun at work.

5. When you are on overload at your work, handling a job designed for two or more persons, you

_____ a. Stress yourself out by doing it anyway.

_____ b. Stress yourself out by not doing it and worrying.

_____ c. Take your stress home and explode on your family until the job gets done.

_____ d. Ask your boss for a meeting to clear up priorities and deadlines on your projects.

6. When you feel a lack of camaraderie on your job, you

_____ a. Sit at your desk and feel sorry for yourself.

_____ b. Keep waiting expectantly for someone to ask you to lunch.

_____ c. Resign yourself to eating alone.

_____ d. Begin developing your network at work by asking people to have lunch or after-hour drinks with you.

7. When you derive no sense of purpose or meaning from your job, you

_____ a. Put in your eight hours, counting the minutes to five o'clock.

_____ b. Find ways to get as many "freebies" as possible from the job to make up for its meaninglessness.

_____ c. Take your job responsibilities less seriously and do only what you have to do to get by.

_____ d. Begin looking for the bigger picture by asking yourself what it is you can learn from that job, what skills you can develop, or what new friends you can make, and how can you make a difference on the job.

As you might have noticed, the last response in each situation is an example of a staying-up behavior. All of the other choices are acting-out behaviors.

Next write down typical pulling-down situations in your job. List your behaviors in each situation. Then go back and check the ones that do not help resolve the problem, that merely express your frustration, or that do not make you feel good about yourself. These are your acting-out behaviors.

| *Pulling-Down Situations* | *My Behaviors* | *Acting-Out* ($\checkmark$) |
|---|---|---|
| 1. _____ | 1. _____ | |
| 2. _____ | 2. _____ | |
| 3. _____ | 3. _____ | |
| 4. _____ | 4. _____ | |
| 5. _____ | 5. _____ | |

Finally, consider whether you have reacted the same way to pulling-down situations in previous jobs. What are some past situations that are similar to the ones you currently face? Which acting-out behaviors did you use to cope? Do any of the same acting-out behaviors you have identified exist in your current job?

What are some staying-up behaviors that helped you cope and that made you feel good about yourself while working to resolve the problem? Are you using these techniques now? How can you incorporate these staying-up behaviors into your current situations?

## FEEDBACK REPORT

Often we are not aware when we are acting out because we are focused on the pulling-down situation that triggered our response. If we have trusted friends and co-workers, we can ask them to help us by answering specific questions. Having other people's feedback can help us analyze our behaviors by becoming aware of how

49

others view us. Stephanie is an example of how the Feedback Report works.

Stephanie, the manager of direct-mail operations, resented her boss for giving her projects with no direction. When Stephanie described her situation, she said, "My boss gives me new projects at the last minute. He never seems to do any long-range planning to do things right. I'm a person who likes to take my time and plan it correctly. I don't like doing things without planning them first."

The next time Stephanie's boss gave her a project, she first did a self-assessment of her reactions and found several acting-out behaviors. Stephanie observed herself saying to her boss, "I don't know if I can get it done by then." Then she went to her desk and began writing a memo to her boss pointing out all the problems she foresaw. Finally she spent most of the afternoon mentally outlining the way she would handle things if she were the boss.

Stephanie then asked a close friend and co-worker to observe her and do a feedback report. The co-worker wrote, "You are a hard worker, and your work is always good. I've noticed, though, that sometimes you don't seem very open to new ideas. I remember one time when all of us were brainstorming some possible solutions to a problem. You found something wrong with all of the solutions! We had to coax you into looking at the possibilities."

This was valuable information for Stephanie. She admitted that sometimes she avoided risk, probably because she wanted to do a perfect job on everything. Stephanie had identified some acting-out behaviors that might be compounding her frustration.

## Your Turn

Listed below are some questions that you can ask trusted friends or co-workers to answer. Be sure to add your own questions that are specific to your job. At the end you will find a list of typical acting-out and staying-up behaviors to help you and others get started.

Use the feedback you receive as you analyze the acting-out behaviors that might be pulling you down.

1. Think of one specific example when I was stressed about something. How did I act? What did I say?
2. What kinds of work situations seem to make me stressed? Who is usually involved—supervisors or co-workers? Do certain work environments bother me, such as noise or lack of privacy? How do I usually cope with these situations—do I try to change things or do I just put up with it?
3. In what ways do I show that I am pleased with something at work? Displeased?
4. How do I react to criticism in my job? Is my reaction to criticism from a supervisor different than it is from a co-worker? How? What are some examples?
5. What methods do I use to handle my stress? What about disappointments? Anger?

6. If I became angry, would you expect me to confront the other person, become silent, tell a supervisor, or complain to my co-workers? What other reactions would you expect?

7. How easy is it for other people to tell what I am feeling? Do I hide my emotions? Or do I wear them on my sleeve? Can you think of examples of why you answered this way?

8. Think about a time when you know I was very happy in my work. How did I act? What did I do or say that was different from when I am unhappy or stressed?

9. If you could choose one word to describe my general behavior on a day-to-day basis, what would it be?

10. What is my response when I am asked to do something? Is my reaction different if the request is made from my supervisor rather than a co-worker? How?

11. How direct am I with other people? Do I say what I mean or do you think I say one thing while feeling another? What are some specific examples?

12. What are some other things about my work behaviors or attitudes that you think might be helpful to me?

The following is a list of typical acting-out and staying-up behaviors. These are just examples to get you thinking.

| *Staying-Up Behaviors* | *Acting-Out Behaviors* |
| --- | --- |
| —cooperating with others | —complaining about boss and co-workers |
| —showing enthusiasm | —lackadaisical attitude about work |
| —apologizing when wrong | —losing temper with co-workers |
| —complimenting others | —criticizing unnecessarily |
| —making light conversation | —spreading hurtful gossip |
| —showing initiative | —waiting until you're told |
| —listening attentively | —being argumentative |
| —being open-minded to new ideas | —being close-minded to ideas |
| —being flexible | —becoming set in own view |
| —creative problem-solving | —doing it the way you always have |
| —showing humor | —showing sour disposition with co-workers |
| —taking initiative | —fearing risk-taking |
| —exuding self-confidence | —feeling powerless on job |
| —skill-building where necessary | —waiting for your boss to initiate things for you |
| —internal sense of control | —feeling out of control |

| Staying-Up Behaviors | Acting-Out Behaviors |
| --- | --- |
| —looking for the big picture | —thinking about self only |
| —showing stability under pressure | —skipping work |
| —working off stress in healthful fashion | —overindulging & bingeing |

## EXPLORE YOUR EARLY MEMORIES

The memories we have of our childhood contain clues that explain our attitudes and behaviors. The tactics we used as children to get attention or to feel important might be similar to our adult responses to situations that threaten us. Let's look at an example of how this works.

Jerry was a program coordinator for a social service agency. This was his story. "I came to this job with high hopes because I seemed to have everything they were looking for. But before long it became clear that my boss wasn't going to give me any important projects. He gave them all to another coordinator. I became very uncomfortable around my boss and had a difficult time making conversation. I really felt like a misfit. Finally I gave up and resigned."

We asked Jerry if he would be willing to analyze his behaviors by looking at his childhood memories. One of the events he described from his childhood particularly impressed us.

"In grade school," Jerry told us, "I was never the

leader, and I was always one of the last to get picked for team sports. It was awful for me to have to wait to see if I would be picked. Several times I ran off the playground or stayed inside the schoolroom during recess."

Jerry's reaction to rejection had followed him from his childhood. When he found himself in a competitive work situation, he "ran away" by quitting his job. In fact, Jerry had not held a job for more than two years at a time. Remembering his childhood reactions helped Jerry to understand and eventually change his current behavior.

## Your Turn

Let's look at some of your early childhood memories. Remember that your purpose is not to blame yourself or others, but to find an understanding of the way you behave in stressful, pulling-down work situations. This understanding will help prepare you to change your acting-out behaviors into staying-up behaviors.

Find a quiet spot and answer these questions as honestly as you can. Be specific in your descriptions.

1. How do you remember yourself as a child?
   a. Were you outgoing or were you reserved around others? Around new people? How about people who were older than you?
   b. Who were your heroes and how did they act?
   c. What were your fears and how did you express them?

    d. How did you respond to criticism? To compliments?

2. Think about the people in your family, both immediate family members and more distant relatives.

    a. Overall, did you come from a positive, accepting family or one in which criticism was more the rule? How did family members react to criticism?

    b. What attitudes and values did your family hold about people, work, and life in general? How did they express these values and attitudes?

    c. Who were your favorite family members? How did they respond to criticism? To stress? To anger?

    d. Try to remember an incident you had with a family member who was in authority. What happened and what was your response? Can you describe how you felt?

    e. What were some of the social or cultural factors that affected your family's reactions? Did people typically speak in soft or loud voices? Adamantly or without expression? With gestures or without?

You should begin to see some basic behavior patterns that began in your childhood. For example, Jill, a 31-year-old clerk-typist, had a history of setting goals that were lower than what she was able to achieve. Jill explained.

"I have a college degree in home economics, but I've never used it. I've always taken the first job that comes along. Then I always get bored six months or so later and I quit. Before long it's the same thing all over."

When Jill explored her childhood memories, she revealed that she had been the youngest in a large family of high-achievers. She was often compared to an older brother or sister.

"I remember always being afraid that I wouldn't do as well," Jill said. "Maybe I thought that if I set low goals for myself, people wouldn't compare me to my brothers and sisters. That way I couldn't fail."

Jill discovered some important information that she was able to use in changing her behavior. She learned to set realistic goals for herself that were challenging but within her reach. She was able to break the cycle of acting-out behaviors.

By analyzing our behaviors, we are taking the first step toward controlling pulling-down situations rather than letting them control us. The honest information we receive from our own and others' observations can guide us toward uncovering sabotaging behavior patterns that we have held over from our childhood.

Now, what is your answer to these questions?

1. Do I need to learn to respond to stressful, pulling-down work situations with productive, staying-up behaviors?
2. Do I want to take responsibility for my own behaviors?

3. Am I ready to change in order to feel better about myself, be more satisfied in my job, and stay up when my job pulls me down?

If your answer to these questions is yes, you are ready to go on to step two of the ADD Strategy: Determine what you *really* want.

# CHAPTER 4

## Step Two: Determine What You Want

FROM OUR YEARS of career counseling, we have come to believe that all of us want three basic things from our work. We want Respect, Responsibility, and Recognition. These ingredients are vital to job satisfaction because they are the ingredients that help us develop and maintain a positive self-concept. When we feel good about ourselves, we feel more accepting of our job. And, when we feel good about our job, we feel good about ourself. Thus, job satisfaction and a positive self-concept are intertwined.

This concept of the relationship between job satisfaction and a positive self-concept can be depicted by conceptualizing a tree that begins growing deep within the earth. (Refer to the illustration on page 60.) Three primary roots become intertwined, creating a trunk. Various branches,

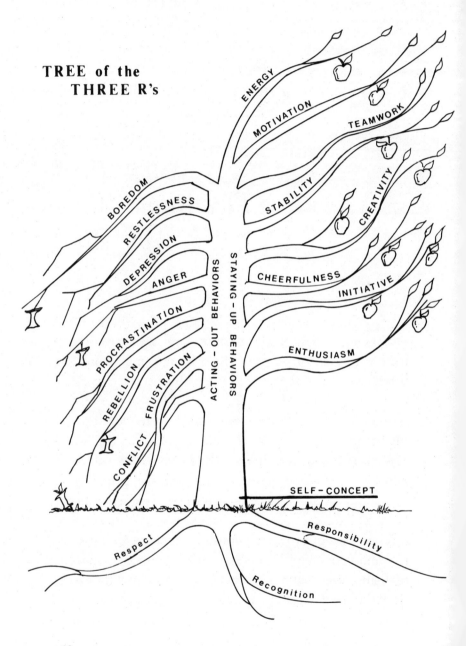

TREE of the THREE R's

ENERGY
MOTIVATION
TEAMWORK
STABILITY
CREATIVITY
CHEERFULNESS
INITIATIVE
ENTHUSIASM

STAYING – UP BEHAVIORS

BOREDOM
RESTLESSNESS
DEPRESSION
ANGER
PROCRASTINATION
REBELLION
CONFLICT FRUSTRATION

ACTING – OUT BEHAVIORS

SELF-CONCEPT

Respect
Responsibility
Recognition

which produce a mixture of fruit, are extended out from the trunk. The fruit from the tree may be sweet or it may be bitter, depending on what the tree has been fed.

We can compare ourselves to the tree, with the three roots representing our inner needs for Respect, Responsibility, and Recognition. These three roots grow together to form the base of the trunk, or our self-concept.

If our self-concept is positive through receiving Respect, Responsibility, and Recognition, we will have productive behaviors that will yield sweet fruit—in other words, productive behaviors which benefit us and those around us.

If, however, our self-concept is smarting, the likelihood is that our behaviors that stem from it will be counterproductive to helping us feel better about ourselves and our job, unless we make a conscious, well-planned effort to avoid falling into a self-defeating cycle of not feeling good about ourself and not feeling good about the job.

## SIGNIFICANCE OF WORK TO A POSITIVE SELF-CONCEPT

If we consider that our work comprises a great portion of our lives, naturally we look to the workplace as a place to fulfill many of the needs that help us maintain a positive self-concept. When the workplace enables us to receive, replenish, and retain the basic ingredients vital to maintaining a positive self-concept, we will experience a greater sense of job satisfaction. But when these basic ingredients are lacking from our work, we experience pulling-down situations.

It is then that we tend to resort to strong responses in efforts to satisfy our basic human need for Respect, Responsibility, and Recognition.

Failure to get Respect, Responsibility, and Recognition needs met is frequently met with behaviors which actually sabotage the very need that we want fulfilled. In such instances, we are acting out, which is not unlike how we acted out as children on the playground.

We don't intentionally sabotage ourselves by resorting to acting-out behaviors. We simply have not mastered the attitudes and skills needed to go after what we want.

From our counseling experience, we believe that what people really want relates back to elements of the Basic Three Rs. Thus, we will approach the second step of the ADD Strategy, Determining what you want, from the perspective of the Three Rs.

Since Respect, Responsibility, and Recognition are crucial to a positive self-concept and to achieving a sense of job satisfaction, we will more fully explore these core ingredients in the next three chapters.

To mentally prepare for these chapters, take a minute to answer these questions. How do you feel when:

1. Your suggestion is brushed aside during a staff meeting?
2. You are not allowed to plan the more mundane aspects of your job?

3. No one mentions the special effort you made on an assignment?
4. Everyone in your department assumes you will cover everyone else's phone?
5. A co-worker repeatedly takes credit for something you both worked on?

In each of these cases our inner needs for the Basic Three Rs are not being met. Our reactions could include anger, frustration, disappointment, hurt, or a number of other feelings. Since we often feel powerless to change the situation, however, we might act out our frustrations with behaviors that further sabotage our Basic Three-R needs.

Chapters 5, 6, and 7 will recount step one of the ADD Strategy: analyzing your behaviors as it takes us into step two: determining what you want. We will look at the various dimensions of each of the Basic Three Rs, using case studies to color our points. We will also generate graphic profiles which explore possible dimensions of each of the Three Rs so that you can visualize which aspects of each of your Basic Three Rs are being met and which of them are weak. This will help you become more focused in specifically determining what you really want.

Finally, in Chapter 8, we will explore step three: Develop an action plan for getting what you want.

# CHAPTER 5

## Respect

### WHAT IS RESPECT AND WHY IS IT IMPORTANT?

THE FIRST ROOT of the Basic Three-R tree is respect. Respect is the affirmation that we are important, worthwhile persons. It is the acknowledgment that, even though we may not be the most gifted, intelligent, or wealthy individual, we still are as important as those who do possess these attributes. We all have a need for this acknowledgment.

Jesse Jackson, a charismatic politician, captured the vision of people's need to feel respected with the simple but poignant phrase, "I am somebody!" He inspired others with a truth that is so fundamental it should be emphasized more. One's spirit cries, "I am somebody!"

Many times we are not aware of the intensity of this need for respect until we experience what it feels like not to be respected. When we do not feel respected, we may experience a wide variety of emotions ranging from humiliation to outrage that can occur when our need for respect is unmet in our work.

## Respect and the Workground

The workground, the place where we spend two-thirds of our lives, is a natural place to seek out this sense of respect. We look for it from our supervisors, co-workers, or subordinates. When we feel respected, it is much easier to maintain staying-up behaviors and to experience a higher level of job satisfaction. When we don't feel as though we are getting the doses of respect that we want, the job sometimes goes sour. So our behaviors go sour, too. A self-defeating cycle begins. The job is not meeting our needs, so we express our needs through acting-out behaviors that actually sabotage our efforts to get what we want. This experience becomes self-perpetuating until we change either our behaviors or our job.

Let's look at examples of how we can sabotage ourselves of respect. Tonya, an administrative assistant, was responsible for coordinating the activities for the board of directors of a large nonprofit organization. This included meeting with the president of the board prior to monthly board meetings.

Each month Tonya would approach the president to schedule the meeting, and each month the president would wait several days before returning her call. In the meantime Tonya was unable to proceed with her work. This not only hampered her schedule, but as she stated, "It makes me feel like I'm not very important—like he wants me to know he outranks me. I think he likes making me wait." Tonya frequently reacted by complaining about the president to co-workers.

Carolyn, the administrative assistant who felt dead-ended by her boss, also sabotaged herself of what she wanted. Carolyn had always appreciated knowing that her staff viewed her as being capable and efficient. They treated her with respect, not just because she was their boss, but because she was competent.

"All of a sudden I noticed that one of my staff seemed to be avoiding me—a young woman who had adopted me as her mentor," Carolyn told us. "I thought I was imagining this at first, but it didn't go away. Sometimes she'd pretend to be busy when I walked by her desk, and she wouldn't look at me when I talked to her."

In reflecting on what happened prior to the times her protégée avoided her, she paused for a moment, sighed, and took a deep breath before continuing. "In all honesty, I noticed that it usually happened after I have snapped at someone."

Carolyn's face displayed the pain of a person who is facing the truth for the first time. "I tried to tell myself she just wasn't as supportive of me as I had thought. But, looking back, I can see that she decided I wasn't worth her admiration. Her body language told me so."

Carolyn was discovering that what she *really* wanted was the sincere respect of her staff, co-workers, and managers. This went further than her desire for a promotion. Her underlying motivation, as with all of us, was the inner need for more respect.

Stan, aged 52, had experienced a phenomenon familiar to many American workers today that further demonstrates our need for respect. His company had decided to eliminate his management job, and he was given the option of taking an early retirement or a lower position. Not feeling that he was ready financially or psychologically to retire, he decided to accept the lower position.

Stan believed he would not find the lower status demeaning. When the job change actually occurred, however, he felt he had lost a strong sense of respect.

One day he saw an acquaintance who also worked for the company in a management position comparable to his old job. She approached him, looked him straight in the eye, and said, "I've never known you too well, Stan, and I don't really know what happened to you, but I just wanted you to know that I've always thought a lot of you and admired your work."

With the words of this co-worker, Stan realized that what he had thought of as respect in his old job was actually just the natural deference people show to those who have position power. He also realized that he had stopped viewing *himself* as being important. The real respect he wanted was there all the time.

## Your Respect Profile

Let's explore the dimensions and degrees of respect that we get on the job. The following are various job characteristics that can pertain to the feeling of being respected.

Read the characteristics and judge the degree to which each one pertains to your job situation. On a scale of 1 to 5, circle the number that best describes how often you feel the characteristic applies to you.

1 = Never   2 = Rarely   3 = Sometimes
4 = Almost Always   5 = Always

| Characteristic | Never | Rarely | Sometimes | Almost Always | Always |
|---|---|---|---|---|---|
| • Co-workers ask for my input when appropriate | 1 | 2 | 3 | 4 | 5 |
| • Supervisors listen to my input about my job | 1 | 2 | 3 | 4 | 5 |
| • Treated with dignity | 1 | 2 | 3 | 4 | 5 |
| • Treated fairly | 1 | 2 | 3 | 4 | 5 |
| • Spoken to in pleasant manner | 1 | 2 | 3 | 4 | 5 |
| • Opportunity to learn new skills | 1 | 2 | 3 | 4 | 5 |
| • Pleasant surroundings | 1 | 2 | 3 | 4 | 5 |

| Characteristic | Never | Rarely | Sometimes | Almost Always | Always |
|---|---|---|---|---|---|
| • Reasonable work schedule | 1 | 2 | 3 | 4 | 5 |
| • Receive answers to my questions | 1 | 2 | 3 | 4 | 5 |
| • Receive training for new job activities | 1 | 2 | 3 | 4 | 5 |
| • Given sufficient information to do job | 1 | 2 | 3 | 4 | 5 |
| • Reasonable workload | 1 | 2 | 3 | 4 | 5 |
| • Can refuse overtime work | 1 | 2 | 3 | 4 | 5 |
| • Feel part of company's mission | 1 | 2 | 3 | 4 | 5 |
| • Work materials or equipment in good condition | 1 | 2 | 3 | 4 | 5 |

## Staying Up When Your Job Pulls You Down

| Characteristic | Never | Rarely | Sometimes | Almost Always | Always |
|---|---|---|---|---|---|
| • Safe working environment | 1 | 2 | 3 | 4 | 5 |
| • Corrected or reprimanded in private | 1 | 2 | 3 | 4 | 5 |
| Other: _____ | 1 | 2 | 3 | 4 | 5 |
| _____ | 1 | 2 | 3 | 4 | 5 |
| _____ | 1 | 2 | 3 | 4 | 5 |

Take a minute to consider why these characteristics are important in affirming workers' sense of respect. Imagine the feeling that comes when these conditions are not present.

No checklist can contain all of the characteristics of a job that reflect respect. You can personalize the profile by listing other job characteristics that might reflect your own ideas about being respected. For example, if having your own private work area signifies respect, include that.

To interpret your profile scores, draw a straight line to connect your circled responses. Then look to see whether the line jogs to the left or to the right. If the line jogs beyond the middle column, toward the left, your job might be lacking in this characteristic; a jog toward the two right-hand columns indicates a possible strength in that respect characteristic.

For example, when Carolyn, who felt dead-ended in her job, saw her responses, she understood that while her respect needs were satisfied in most ways, she did not feel her supervisors or her co-workers listened to important information she thought she was entitled to give. Also, she felt overloaded with work and did not see how her own work fit into the overall goals of the company. Carolyn's Respect Profile looked like this.

## CAROLYN'S RESPECT PROFILE

| Characteristic | Never | Rarely | Sometimes | Almost Always | Always |
|---|---|---|---|---|---|
| • Co-workers ask for my input when appropriate | 1 | ②| 3 | 4 | 5 |
| • Supervisors listen to my input about my job | 1 | ② | 3 | 4 | 5 |
| • Treated with dignity | 1 | 2 | 3 | ④ | 5 |
| • Treated fairly | 1 | 2 | 3 | ④ | 5 |

## CAROLYN'S RESPECT PROFILE (*cont.*)

| Characteristic | Never | Rarely | Sometimes | Almost Always | Always |
|---|---|---|---|---|---|
| • Spoken to in pleasant manner | 1 | 2 | 3 | ④ | 5 |
| • Opportunity to learn new skills | 1 | 2 | 3 | 4 | ⑤ |
| • Pleasant surroundings | 1 | 2 | 3 | 4 | ⑤ |
| • Reasonable work schedule | 1 | 2 | ③ | 4 | 5 |
| • Receive answers to my questions | 1 | 2 | 3 | ④ | 5 |
| • Receive training for new job activities | 1 | 2 | 3 | ④ | 5 |
| • Given sufficient information to do job | 1 | 2 | 3 | ④ | 5 |
| • Reasonable workload | 1 | 2 | ③ | 4 | 5 |

| Characteristic | Never | Rarely | Sometimes | Almost Always | Always |
|---|---|---|---|---|---|
| • Can refuse overtime work | 1 | ② | 3 | 4 | 5 |
| • Feel part of company's mission | ① | 2 | 3 | 4 | 5 |
| • Work materials or equipment in good condition | 1 | 2 | 3 | ④ | 5 |
| • Safe working environment | 1 | 2 | 3 | 4 | ⑤ |
| • Corrected or reprimanded in private | 1 | 2 | 3 | 4 | ⑤ |
| Other: _____ | 1 | 2 | 3 | 4 | 5 |
| _____ | 1 | 2 | 3 | 4 | 5 |
| _____ | 1 | 2 | 3 | 4 | 5 |

We can start to understand what our respect needs are and more clearly determine what we want by examining our responses to this exercise. When Carolyn connected her responses with straight lines, she found several severe dips in her Respect Profile. Looking at those characteris-

tics that she rated as being a 1 or a 2, she found herself
lacking respect in these instances:

| Characteristic | Never | Rarely | Sometimes | Almost Always | Always |
|---|---|---|---|---|---|
| • Co-workers ask for my input when appropriate | 1 | ②| 3 | 4 | 5 |
| • Supervisors listen to my input about my job | 1 | ② | 3 | 4 | 5 |
| • Can refuse overtime work | 1 | ② | 3 | 4 | 5 |
| • Feel part of company's mission | ① | 2 | 3 | 4 | 5 |

In general Carolyn felt that if she were truly respected,
her co-workers would ask for her input on projects that
her work impacted. Likewise, the company managers
would seek her opinion if she were really contributing to
the firm's mission. Once Carolyn acknowledged her respect needs, she was ready to begin developing an action
plan to get what she really wanted.

Likewise, to help Stan accept his new position, he
needed to look at himself truthfully and acknowledge

that the real issue was that he needed to reaffirm his sense of respect.

A client who finally came to this realization was David, an engineer in a large consulting company.

David had a co-worker who attempted to get attention for himself by belittling David—denying him respect.

"He only does it when there's a whole group of people around," David told us. "Usually he criticizes the way I've done something. Sometimes he actually shouts. I can't go to my boss because one time my co-worker started in on how I played up to the boss. You can just imagine how that made me look to everyone. But I really want to keep this job. The salary is okay, and it's close to my house. Also, I don't have to travel—which helps out since my wife has gone back to college."

Finally we believed we had gotten to the real problem. David had allowed his co-worker to control a very important part of his self-concept—respect. David felt that because the co-worker spoke in such a disrespectful way, it meant that the other staff members didn't respect him either. He began viewing himself as being a person who was not respected. This was devastating to David's self-concept.

David had no control over his co-worker, but he could look at what he himself might change in order to view himself more positively. In fact, the only thing that David *could* control was his own behaviors. Here are the first two steps David lined out in his ADD Strategy.

## Step One: Analyze Your Behaviors

When David explored his early memories, he realized that he had viewed respect as being symbolized by a person in a professional position. David's parents had been hardworking people who led a simple life in order to provide a college education for their children. Teachers, doctors, clergy—all were professional people whom David's parents had looked up to, and they taught their children to do the same. David wanted to be respected like that too when he became an adult.

David had assumed that everyone would treat professionals with respect, as his parents had done. Thus, when his co-worker attempted to belittle him, David first reacted with disbelief, then with humiliation, then with anger. Since he rarely confronted anyone with his anger, he allowed his feelings to come out in acting-out behaviors that expressed his frustrations but that did not address the problem.

David was able to see that his co-worker was really no different from a childhood bully who tried to make himself seem important by pushing the other kids around.

David also analyzed his behavior by doing a behavior self-assessment. His wife and a co-worker helped him identify acting-out behaviors by giving him feedback from their observations. Together they pieced together the following pattern.

In an effort to avoid losing his temper and foolishly quitting his job, David had developed a passive response that he did not respect. He would stay at his desk with his head down. This behavior made him feel disappointed in himself, as if he were a child who had run away.

David also complained to his wife, and he was afraid that this made him dwell on the incident even more. Finally, he had developed the habit of purposely setting up situations that would put the co-worker in a bad light, such as failing to deliver messages or other information. While this method of retaliation never had serious consequences, it nonetheless contributed to David's negative self-concept. It might even have aggravated his co-worker's temper.

How did David come to the realization that he did not respect his behaviors? Since David's co-worker was as antagonistic toward other people in the office as he was with David, we had him examine his reactions to the way other people behaved in this situation. This often is a helpful technique because it is easier to pinpoint our reactions to other people's behaviors than it is to pinpoint our own.

First David listed the behaviors of several of his co-workers. Then he identified whether or not he respected each behavior.

| Person's Name | Description of Behavior | My Reactions: Respect or Don't Respect |
|---|---|---|
| 1. Tina | Snaps back at him | Don't respect |
| 2. Hank | Cracks a joke | Respect |
| 3. Jacob | Goes to his desk | Don't respect |
| 4. Gene | Tells the boss | Don't respect |
| 5. Wanda | Ignores him | Respect |

David did not respect the behaviors of his co-workers Tina, Jacob, and Gene because he thought that snapping back did not accomplish anything. Staying at a desk was too passive, and reporting the incident to the boss did not help.

When David realized that his behavior was the same as Jacob's, he could understand why he felt so dejected. Just as he did not respect Jacob for passively staying at his desk, so he did not respect himself.

With this new understanding of his acting-out behaviors, David was ready to go on to step two and determine what he really wanted.

### Step Two: Determine What You Really Want

In order to help David more clearly determine what he wanted, we first had him complete a Respect Profile.

Next we helped him consider how he might be using staying-up or acting-out behaviors that supported or sabotaged his need for a sense of respect.

First David listed the acting-out behaviors he had identified and analyzed. Then he briefly described how each behavior further depleted the sense of respect in his self-concept, the very thing he wanted most. His answers are on the following form.

| *Description of Acting-Out Behavior* | *How This Sabotages My Sense of Respect* |
|---|---|
| Hide at my desk | I don't respect it |
| Hang my head | Makes me feel unworthy |
| Complain to my wife | Makes me dwell on it |
| Set up situations to make him look bad | This is really low— makes me feel guilty |

David eventually went on to develop an action plan that was successful in nourishing his self-concept by increasing his sense of respect. He developed new, staying-up behaviors that allowed him to reframe the way he viewed himself.

He discovered that no one can strip us of respect. We each are human beings, and as such are important and worthwhile. No one can take those qualities from us; we take them from ourselves.

**Your Turn**

You can use steps one and two of the ADD Strategy as David did to help you analyze your behaviors and more clearly determine what it is you really want. When you analyzed your early memories, what were some of your childhood lessons in respect? What feedback did co-workers and friends give you about your behaviors? What were the needs you identified on your Respect Profile?

Can you think of ways to structure your job that would make you feel more respected?

In order to become more aware of the role of respect in your job situation and to determine your respect needs and desires, it is helpful to consider other people who are having job problems similar to yours.

Write the names of these people in the column on the left. In the middle column, briefly describe the people's behaviors. Then decide whether or not you respect each behavior. Your list might look something like David's.

| Person's Name | Description of Behavior | My Reactions: Respect or Don't Respect |
|---|---|---|
| 1. | | |
| 2. | | |
| 3. | | |
| 4. | | |
| 5. | | |

Are your behaviors similar to those of anyone else on your list? What is the behavior, and whose is it? Is it a behavior you respect or do not respect?

Next use the following format to describe how you might be sabotaging your own sense of respect with acting-out behaviors. Write the acting-out behaviors you identified in the left-hand column and then briefly describe how you might be keeping yourself from getting the respect you really want.

| *Description of Acting-Out Behavior* | *How This Sabotages My Sense of Respect* |
|---|---|
| 1. _____ | 1. _____ |
| 2. _____ | 2. _____ |
| 3. _____ | 3. _____ |
| 4. _____ | 4. _____ |
| 5. _____ | 5. _____ |

All of us can become aware of respect and understand that we might be sabotaging this need through our own acting-out behaviors. We must begin to acknowledge that *real* respect starts from inside and works out.

We can learn to change our counterproductive behaviors and to affirm ourselves as being important. Our feelings of self-respect will then enhance our job satisfaction.

# Chapter 6

# *Responsibility*

## What Is Responsibility and Why Is It Important?

The second root of the Basic Three-R Tree is responsibility. As with respect, becoming more aware of responsibility in our everyday lives helps us to understand why it is important.

At the center of responsibility is the opportunity to make decisions and to feel more of a sense of control over our lives. This decision-making opportunity and sense of control is empowering to our self-concept. It allows us to feel more like victors than victims. Feeling a sense of responsibility also validates our sense of competence and feelings of our own worth. Whenever we are required to be accountable for the choice between two or more alternatives, we have responsibility, great or small.

## Responsibility and the Workground

Many people anticipate receiving increased responsibility the longer they have been in a job. The anticipation is usually thought of in terms of promotions. When we are not promoted into a higher position, we might feel something is wrong with us. We might even believe that our supervisors do not consider us to be trustworthy.

For example, Cynthia was a typist in a typing pool. She was an efficient and fast typist who frequently trained new typists. She knew her performance was good, she received top salary increases, yet she hadn't received a promotion into what she considered to be a more responsible position. While Cynthia wanted a promotion, she was able to reframe her perception of responsibility to see that there are many levels of responsibility. She trained other typists, and supervisors came to her for special and urgent typing projects. She was recognized in the typing pool as an expert.

## Your Responsibility Profile

Like Cynthia, all of us have a mental image of what responsibility should be. Also, like Cynthia we can identify some basic work conditions that contribute to our sense of responsibility.

Do you have the opportunity to make decisions in your job? What choices do you make that fill your need for responsibility? Complete the following exercise to develop an individual profile of your responsibility needs.

Listed below are job characteristics that pertain to the feeling of having responsibility. Read the characteristics and judge the degree to which each one pertains to your job situation. On a scale of 1 to 5, circle the number that best describes how often you feel that the characteristic applies to you.

1 = Never   2 = Rarely   3 = Sometimes
4 = Almost Always   5 = Always

| Characteristic | Never | Rarely | Sometimes | Almost Always | Always |
|---|---|---|---|---|---|
| • Choice between at least two methods for completing work activities | 1 | 2 | 3 | 4 | 5 |
| • Authority to change or add work activities as necessary | 1 | 2 | 3 | 4 | 5 |
| • Expected to complete work activities with minimum supervision | 1 | 2 | 3 | 4 | 5 |

| Characteristic | Never | Rarely | Sometimes | Almost Always | Always |
|---|---|---|---|---|---|
| • Opportunity to initiate new work activities | 1 | 2 | 3 | 4 | 5 |
| • Well-defined work activities | 1 | 2 | 3 | 4 | 5 |
| • Work activities are clearly important to company's objectives | 1 | 2 | 3 | 4 | 5 |
| • Opportunity to see results or outcomes of work activities | 1 | 2 | 3 | 4 | 5 |
| • Work activities require use of multiple skills | 1 | 2 | 3 | 4 | 5 |
| • Opportunity to solve problems | 1 | 2 | 3 | 4 | 5 |

## Staying Up When Your Job Pulls You Down

| Characteristic | Never | Rarely | Sometimes | Almost Always | Always |
|---|---|---|---|---|---|
| • Authority to make judgments about quality of work | 1 | 2 | 3 | 4 | 5 |
| • Results of work activities impact other employees' work or customers' lives | 1 | 2 | 3 | 4 | 5 |
| • Opportunity to give input into overall company objectives | 1 | 2 | 3 | 4 | 5 |
| • Authority to arrange work station somewhat to facilitate job | 1 | 2 | 3 | 4 | 5 |
| • Accountable for accuracy of work | 1 | 2 | 3 | 4 | 5 |

| Characteristic | Never | Rarely | Sometimes | Almost Always | Always |
|---|---|---|---|---|---|
| • Expected to share information with co-workers when appropriate | 1 | 2 | 3 | 4 | 5 |
| • Complexity of work activities equal to skill level | 1 | 2 | 3 | 4 | 5 |
| • Expected to maintain skills required for work activities | 1 | 2 | 3 | 4 | 5 |
| • Accountable for supervising the work of others | 1 | 2 | 3 | 4 | 5 |
| Other: _____ | 1 | 2 | 3 | 4 | 5 |
| _____ | 1 | 2 | 3 | 4 | 5 |
| _____ | 1 | 2 | 3 | 4 | 5 |

Pause for a moment to think about the job characteristics that are listed in this exercise. Are you able to identify why they represent responsibility? Two basic examples are being able to choose between at least two methods of completing your work and to do so with little supervision. Without these, you might feel that you have little responsibility in your work.

Likewise, being expected to share appropriate information with your co-workers, performing work activities that are at least equal to your skill level, and being accountable for your work accuracy are examples of common job characteristics that give workers a sense that their work is important—that they have a responsible position. Can you think of other job characteristics that signify responsibility to you? Whether or not these currently are part of your job, add them to the list of characteristics to personalize the checklist.

To interpret your profile scores, draw a straight line to connect your circled responses. Then look to see whether the line jogs to the left or to the right. If the line jogs beyond the middle column, toward the left, your job might be lacking in this characteristic; a jog toward the two right-hand columns indicates a possible strength in that respect characteristic.

Carolyn, the administrative assistant who felt dead-ended, was entrusted with a great deal of responsibility. However, because her boss took credit for her ideas, no one knew how responsible she really was. The more angry Carolyn became and the more she brooded over the problem in her office, the more she began to neglect her responsibilities. This had been bothering her for some time.

"I have always believed that supervisors need to be out in the office area, seeing what is happening, rather than being holed up in their own office space. So many things occur that shouldn't just because some managers fail to take responsibility to find out what is going on."

Carolyn had formed a picture of the ideal supervisor in her mind. Thus, when Carolyn's problems caused her to become "immobilized," she found that the picture she had of the ideal supervisor no longer matched the picture she had of herself. Instead she had begun to see herself as an ineffective manager who did not take responsibility.

Carolyn needed to reframe her understanding of responsibility. Ultimately, it really didn't matter whether her boss or her staff considered her to be a responsible person. In her own mind, she had been given a duty, and she was abdicating that responsibility. This affected her self-concept.

When Carolyn completed her profile, she found that she had more responsibility in her current job than she had thought, but not as much as she wanted. She also discovered that the areas in which she lacked a sense of responsibility were ones that she could compensate for herself. Carolyn's Responsibility Profile follows.

## CAROLYN'S RESPONSIBILITY PROFILE

| Characteristic | Never | Rarely | Sometimes | Almost Always | Always |
|---|---|---|---|---|---|
| • Choice between at least two methods for completing work activities | 1 | 2 | 3 | ④ | 5 |
| • Authority to change or add work activities as necessary | 1 | 2 | 3 | ④ | 5 |
| • Expected to complete work activities with minimum supervision | 1 | 2 | 3 | 4 | ⑤ |
| • Opportunity to initiate new work activities | 1 | 2 | 3 | 4 | ⑤ |

| Characteristic | Never | Rarely | Sometimes | Almost Always | Always |
|---|---|---|---|---|---|
| • Well-defined work activities | 1 | 2 | 3 | ④ | 5 |
| • Work activities are clearly important to company's objectives | 1 | ② | 3 | 4 | 5 |
| • Opportunity to see results or outcomes of work activities | 1 | ② | 3 | 4 | 5 |
| • Work activities require use of multiple skills | 1 | 2 | 3 | ④ | 5 |
| • Opportunity to solve problems | 1 | 2 | 3 | 4 | ⑤ |
| • Authority to make judgments about quality of work | 1 | 2 | 3 | ④ | 5 |

## CAROLYN'S RESPONSIBILITY PROFILE *(cont.)*

| Characteristic | Never | Rarely | Sometimes | Almost Always | Always |
|---|---|---|---|---|---|
| • Results of work activities impact other employees' work or customers' lives | 1 | ②| 3 | 4 | 5 |
| • Opportunity to give input into overall company objectives | ① | 2 | 3 | 4 | 5 |
| • Authority to arrange work station somewhat to facilitate job | 1 | 2 | 3 | 4 | ⑤ |
| • Accountable for accuracy of work | 1 | 2 | 3 | 4 | ⑤ |
| • Expected to share information | 1 | ② | 3 | 4 | 5 |

92

| Characteristic | Never | Rarely | Sometimes | Almost Always | Always |
|---|---|---|---|---|---|
| with co-workers when appropriate | | | | | |
| • Complexity of work activities equal to skill level | 1 | 2 | 3 | ④ | 5 |
| • Expected to maintain skills required for work activities | 1 | 2 | 3 | 4 | ⑤ |
| • Accountable for supervising the work of others | 1 | 2 | 3 | 4 | ⑤ |
| Other: _____ | 1 | 2 | 3 | 4 | 5 |
| _____ | 1 | 2 | 3 | 4 | 5 |
| _____ | 1 | 2 | 3 | 4 | 5 |

Carolyn was able to get a good visual of some of her responsibility needs by connecting straight lines

to her responses. There were several instances where
the line jogged to the left of the middle column on the
scale.

| Characteristic | Never | Rarely | Sometimes | Almost Always | Always |
|---|---|---|---|---|---|
| • Work activities are clearly important to company's objectives | 1 | ②| 3 | 4 | 5 |
| • Opportunity to see results or outcomes of work activities | 1 | ② | 3 | 4 | 5 |
| • Results of work activities impact other employees' work or customers' lives | 1 | ② | 3 | 4 | 5 |
| • Opportunity to give input into overall company objectives | ① | 2 | 3 | 4 | 5 |

| Characteristic | Never | Rarely | Sometimes | Almost Always | Always |
|---|---|---|---|---|---|
| • Expected to share information with co-workers when appropriate | 1 | ② | 3 | 4 | 5 |

When Carolyn saw the results of this exercise, she began to understand why she sometimes felt as though others might not consider her to be trustworthy or responsible. She had little understanding of how her work fit into the goals of the company, she usually was not aware of the results or outcome of her projects, and she did not know to what extent her work impacted the work of others. This was information Carolyn could discover for herself, thus increasing her sense of responsibility.

Another client of ours who learned to add responsibility to her self-concept was Judy, the office manager for the loan department of a large bank. Judy was a woman in her early forties who had returned to work several years earlier after having been a full-time homemaker. Let's look at Judy's story.

Judy had been happy in her job until recently, when she began noticing that it was not giving her the satisfaction it once had. Yet Judy did not want to leave her company; she had two children who were in college, and she appreciated the apparent security of her current employer.

Judy's specific problem was her frustration over not having enough responsibility in her job.

"I worked my way up to being office manager," Judy told us when she came to talk about changing jobs. "I'm really proud of that, because I started as a typist. I had to go to night school since I worked all day, and it wasn't easy. I report directly to the credit department manager. I had a good relationship with the manager who hired me. But he left, and the woman they put in there about six months ago doesn't like me."

Judy was obviously proud of her accomplishments; she was a person who had eagerly taken opportunities for responsibility when they were assigned to her.

Judy seemed so sure, however, that her supervisor didn't like her. Yet when we asked Judy why she thought this, she responded, "She tells me exactly how to do everything. She goes into very minute detail about every little thing she asks me to do. It's plain that she thinks I couldn't do it without very explicit instructions. Sometimes I wonder if she might be right."

Judy suddenly sounded very unsure of herself. She seemed to have some doubts about her own skills. Judy had become so frustrated, in fact, that she was considering requesting a transfer to a position in another department in the company, even though this would have meant taking a lower position.

At this point we suggested that Judy might want to

consider some career counseling rather than proceeding with her job search. We pointed out to her that if she were to transfer to another department, she might be faced with the same dilemma before too long. Perhaps there was another way to work out the problem rather than going to another department and starting out all over again. Let's look at how Judy used step one and step two of the ADD Strategy to analyze her behavior and to determine what she really wanted.

## Step One: Analyze Your Behaviors

First Judy looked at her early childhood memories. They included several significant things that might have affected the way she felt about responsibility. She had grown up in a very traditional family where the women were full-time homemakers. The men made the decisions and bore the responsibility for taking care of the family.

Judy remembered that whenever she wanted something, her mother usually answered, "We'll have to ask your father." It seemed to Judy that she might have developed some rigid ideas about responsibility, believing that one person makes the decision and gives permission while someone else carries out the decision. This concept gave Judy problems in a work situation where taking, or initiating, responsibility is necessary.

Judy examined these early memories to identify possible acting-out behaviors that she might still be using. She also asked friends and co-workers to observe her and give her feedback about what behaviors might be depleting her sense of responsibility. While Judy discovered that others thought she appeared loyal and anxious to do a good job, she also discovered her responses to her job frustrations were predictable.

Judy had developed a pattern of acting-out behaviors that helped her cope with the immediate situation but that did nothing to solve the overall problem. For example, because she was insecure about her own skills, Judy sat back and did not tell her new supervisor what activities she had performed independently in the past. Instead, she waited for her supervisor to give her instructions.

Additionally, Judy did not speak up when her supervisor had a question she thought she could answer; instead she pretended she did not know for fear of being wrong. Likewise, Judy did not trust her own judgment to tell her supervisor about ineffective office procedures, even though her judgment about these had always been very good.

Finally, while Judy still distributed projects, she did not follow up on them as she had in the past. Instead, she decided that she should wait until her supervisor instructed her to do so, even though it was part of her job description.

Judy did not have bad intentions; she did not intend to appear uncooperative. She merely doubted her own skills. Her supervisor, however, mistook her lack of initiative as being lack of ability and an unwillingness to accept responsibility and began giving Judy detailed instructions. Judy interpreted this to mean her supervisor did not like her, and a cycle was started that came to perpetuate itself.

Finally, as part of her behavior self-assessment, we had Judy complete some open-ended statements about the decisions she made in her job. In this way she could see how her own acting-out behaviors were part of the problem.

The statements and Judy's answers follow.

1. Some of my current job responsibilities are:
   a. Distribute office projects;
   b. Devise and implement procedures for tracking progress of projects;
   c. Oversee operations of office.
2. Examples of decisions I make are:
   a. When to report to my supervisor that a project isn't being done properly;
   b. I don't make any other decisions at this time, although I used to.
3. The decisions that make me feel most responsible are:
   a. None—it's not difficult reporting to my supervisor if something isn't getting done!
4. The decisions that make me feel least responsible are:
   a. Telling my supervisor when a project is behind.
5. Instead, these decisions make me feel _____ because:
   a. Untrustworthy—like my supervisor can't trust me to see that projects are done right and on time.

99

As we can see from her answers, Judy felt she was no longer required to make decisions, and she used the word "untrustworthy" to describe the way she thought her supervisor viewed her. This choice of words demonstrated to Judy that whether her supervisor liked her or not was not the issue. More important was the fact that Judy's acting-out behaviors caused her supervisor to view her as being irresponsible.

Further, Judy saw that she had given up control of activities she had performed in the past. Finally, Judy's analysis of her behavior revealed that she even had stopped viewing herself as being a responsible person.

## Step Two: Determine What You Really Want

In order to help Judy focus on what she really wanted, we had her complete a Responsibility Profile. From her responses, Judy discovered that her dissatisfaction appeared to stem from the fact that she felt she did not have adequate freedom and latitude to solve problems. She described herself as being supervised closely, with little authority to express judgments or institute changes. She did not even view herself as being accountable for the accuracy of the work, though technically she was the manager of the office.

Yet, as Judy herself pointed out, this had not always been the case. Her previous supervisor had entrusted the entire operation of the office to her. At this point Judy began to make the connection between her own failure to initiate responsibility and her current job dissatisfaction.

Judy realized that her low-risk behavior had protected her from possible failure but had robbed her of the sense of responsibility she wanted.

Next we had Judy look more specifically at how she might be sabotaging her own sense of responsibility. It was true that Judy's strong need for responsibility motivated her to move into better-paying positions. However, it also was true that her insecurities led her to cope with pulling-down situations through acting-out behaviors that sabotaged her from getting the very thing that she wanted—responsibility. She completed the following chart.

| *Description of Acting-Out Behavior* | *How This Sabotages My Sense of Responsibility* |
|---|---|
| 1. Sit back instead of solving problems | 1. Looks like I won't cooperate |
| 2. Wait to be told what to do | 2. Don't appear to be a self-starter |
| 3. Pretend I don't know the answer | 3. But I do! I should be proud |
| 4. Don't report ineffective office procedures | 4. This used to be my strong point |
| 5. Don't follow up on projects I distribute | 5. It's my job—makes me look incompetent |

Once Judy had completed this exercise, she discovered what was bothering her—she did not feel that she was accountable for anything. In short, Judy did not feel she had enough responsibility. Furthermore, her insecurities had caused her to abdicate the few responsibilities she actually had.

Like Judy, many of us sabotage our own sense of responsibility with acting-out behaviors that help us cope with frustrations but that are ineffective in solving problems. We sometimes give an impression opposite from what we intended. When this happens it might not be long before we actually *are* left out of decisions and start to view ourselves as being untrustworthy.

## Your Turn

How about you? What was the first lesson you can remember in responsibility? Is it possible that some of your current behaviors are remnants of your childhood? After getting some feedback from co-workers and friends, identify your acting-out behaviors and describe how they might be sabotaging your need for a sense of responsibility. What behaviors would make you feel responsible? Can you think of ways to meet the needs you identified on your Responsibility Profile?

In order to understand how responsibility motivates you, try to become more aware of the role of responsibility in your job. Take a few minutes to answer the questions that Judy asked herself. List some of the activities you enjoy about your job—and some you do not enjoy. Also include some activities that are listed in your job description and others that you do voluntarily.

1. Some of my current job responsibilities are:

   a.

   b.

   c.

   d.

   e.

2. Examples of decisions I make are:

   a.

   b.

   c.

   d.

   e.

3. The decisions that make me feel most responsible are:

   a.

   b.

   c.

4. The decisions that make me feel least responsible are:

   a.

   b.

   c.

5. Instead, these decisions make me feel _____ because:

   a.

   b.

   c.

Were you surprised at the number of decisions you made? Which decisions do you respond to with behaviors that do not make you feel responsible?

Next, describe how your acting-out behaviors might be working to sabotage the sense of responsibility you want. Complete the following form.

| *Description of Acting-Out Behavior* | *How This Sabotages My Sense of Responsibility* |
| --- | --- |
| 1. _____ | 1. _____ |
| 2. _____ | 2. _____ |
| 3. _____ | 3. _____ |
| 4. _____ | 4. _____ |
| 5. _____ | 5. _____ |

No job duty is insignificant enough that there cannot be some choice in how we perform it. No one can perform our tasks like we can. They are expressions of ourselves. When we look within to create opportunities to make decisions rather than waiting for someone else to dictate our choices, we develop control over our own activities. By creating alternatives and being accountable for the results of our decisions, we prove that we are trustworthy and increase the sense of responsibility needed for a positive self-concept.

# CHAPTER 7

## Recognition

### WHAT IS RECOGNITION AND WHY IS IT IMPORTANT?

RECOGNITION IS THE flame that sparks and energizes our spirits. While we often think of recognition as being a reward for doing something well, the power of recognition is far more than that. As the third root of the Basic Three-R Tree, recognition provides the necessary nourishment for a healthy trunk. It strengthens a healthy self-concept by validating our status as responsible people worthy of respect. Our basic human nature wants attention and praise.

Recognition is the affirmation of our individuality. When we are recognized as standing apart from others, we know that we are unique or special in some way. Each of us has a deep need for this acknowledgment; it forms the basis for our belief that we can make a difference in the world through our work.

Most of us would agree that when we have this appreciation for the work we do, we are more satisfied with our job.

Likewise, many of us find it *un*motivating when our efforts are *not* acknowledged and we remain an unidentified member of the group. It might make us feel as if our hard work has been worthless. For example, Carolyn felt that her boss took the credit for her ideas.

"I feel like I've been throwing myself at a brick wall," Carolyn told us. "I think up all these great ideas and I get my boss enthusiastic about them. And they always work. But that's the end of it."

When we asked Carolyn if she could tell us what she wished her boss would do, she answered, "Yes, I can give you a very specific example. One day my friend's supervisor was talking about her in the company cafeteria. The supervisor told some of the other department heads about a new procedure used in her department for speeding up the time between a customer's order and the delivery. I heard her tell them that it had been Fran's idea—she said that she really hadn't thought of it before, but when Fran brought it up, it all made so much sense to her."

Carolyn obviously felt that her friend's supervisor does what good supervisors should do—give their staff credit. It was very rewarding to Carolyn to have her ideas recognized, and when that did not happen she reacted by becoming less enthusiastic. She withdrew to her office and became despondent.

Each time this happened, Carolyn eventually mustered the effort to talk herself into becoming involved once more. "I develop another idea and tell my boss about it; he thinks it's a great idea; and then that's the last I ever hear about me! The next thing I know, I'm hearing from other people about *his* idea! The same thing happens all over again. I'm sick of it!"

Like Carolyn, many of us feel at times that we are not appreciated. Our hard work often goes unnoticed, while others might seem to get away with doing only half as much. Like Carolyn, too, most of us do not require a promotion, a raise, or another large reward in order to feel recognized. Just knowing that others are aware of our efforts is often sufficient recognition.

## Understanding Recognition

As with respect and responsibility, recognition is a great deal more than it seems on the surface. In order to determine our needs, and thus what we really want, we must explore beneath this surface and develop a deeper understanding of recognition.

There are two types of recognition in our work— formal and informal. Raises, promotions, and letters of commendation are examples of formal recognition. While everyone likes to be recognized in these ways, informal recognition is also important.

Informal recognition is a reward for just being ourselves. It is bestowed through such actions as a thank-you letter, a hello, a smile, or even by a nod of the head. All of us have had the experience of walking into a meeting or the lunch room and having someone recognize us from a previous occasion. We feel flattered that we have been remembered and noticed.

Likewise, many of us know how it feels to begin a job with a new company and to be unrecognized by other people. We hope that people will remember our name and come to know some of our unique characteristics—in short, to recognize us. When no one knows us, we tend to feel that we blend into the crowd and that there is nothing special about us. None of us like feeling this way.

People come to recognize us by those individual characteristics that make us different from others. Perhaps it is a sense of humor, a manner of speaking, or a way of dressing. Can you remember co-workers whom others came to know because of their cheerful smile or the uplifting sound of their voice? Or people who are known and recognized for their gruffness? These are characteristics that others tend to remember.

The degree that we are recognizable depends to a large extent upon our visibility. A woman in one of our career-planning workshops told us that she had become dissatisfied in her job when her work station had been moved to a spot where she sat with her back to the door, facing a wall. At first she did not realize what was bothering her. She only knew that she had become unhappy.

Finally she determined that she missed being visible—

having people who came into the office see her and having the ability to look up and see them. While she didn't actually greet people as part of her job duties, she missed recognizing people and having them recognize her. When she requested having her work station turned around so that she faced toward the people entering the office rather than toward the wall, her outlook improved remarkably.

Learning to be visible also became an important lesson for Carolyn. When Carolyn withdrew to her office, she not only was shirking her responsibilities, but she was keeping others from knowing her. Carolyn needed to become visible, meet new people, and promote herself rather than relying on her boss to meet all of her recognition needs.

## Recognition and the Workground

All of us have the desire to be set apart, to be considered as an individual, to be recognized. This is only human. It is precisely because we *are* human that we strive to fulfill our potential and to reach for something better. These qualities come to us naturally as human beings, no matter who we are.

Many of us have been led to believe that people in high positions are more recognizable. Certainly they may be known to more people in the company simply due to their high visibility. This form of recognition, though, does not necessarily mean that these people are more appreciated. An example of this misconception is the case of Allen.

Allen was the catalogue-production coordinator for a large retail company. It was his job to coordinate all aspects of the quarterly catalogue, including the advertising copy and photography. While he was not ultimately responsible for the production budget, he was expected to use cost-effective techniques. All of this had to happen within strict deadlines.

Obviously this was a high-pressure job. Allen seemed well matched to the task, though. He appeared to have a high level of energy, talking with conviction and expressively.

"I do all of this," Allen said, "without anyone hanging over me. I love it. I get to travel, talk with the people who provide the models, interact with the different departments, get to know all the technicians. But the department heads think they do it all, even though every time I go into the lounge they're all in there drinking coffee. Without me, though, that catalogue wouldn't come off on time and there would be lots of hassle for them. They just don't know it."

Allen understandably felt that he didn't get enough recognition for this important job. Further, he felt the department heads probably believed his job wasn't really that important. Allen had become focused on this lack of attention, and he had come to view himself as not being appreciated.

During the rest of the workshop, however, we discovered that Allen literally received more phone calls than anyone else in the company, including the president. This was because he was the contact person for the outside firms that contracted to do specialized jobs for the catalogue. In this sense Allen was more recognized than anyone else!

Eventually Allen came to see that he needed to find other ways to affirm his need for recognition. He learned to become more aware of many forms of recognition. Also, he came to reframe the way he viewed attention; although he was not recognized as having one of the highest positions in the company, he came to acknowledge that he received other kinds of recognition.

## Your Recognition Profile

How much opportunity do you have in your job for recognition? Are large rewards such as a promotion or a raise the only forms of recognition that are meaningful to you? Or is it also rewarding to have people know you and your name? Complete the following Recognition Profile to develop a personalized profile of your recognition needs.

Listed are job characteristics that pertain to the feeling of being recognized. Read the characteristics, and judge the degree to which each characteristic pertains to your job situation. On a scale of 1 to 5, circle the number that best describes how often you feel that the characteristic applies to you.

## Staying Up When Your Job Pulls You Down

1 = Never    2 = Rarely    3 = Sometimes
4 = Almost Always    5 = Always

| Characteristic | Never | Rarely | Sometimes | Almost Always | Always |
|---|---|---|---|---|---|
| • Physically visible to co-workers or public | 1 | 2 | 3 | 4 | 5 |
| • Frequent communication with co-workers | 1 | 2 | 3 | 4 | 5 |
| • Frequent communication with supervisors | 1 | 2 | 3 | 4 | 5 |
| • Frequent communication with other people, e.g., clients | 1 | 2 | 3 | 4 | 5 |
| • Name is used in process of work activities, e.g., on | 1 | 2 | 3 | 4 | 5 |

| Characteristic | Never | Rarely | Sometimes | Almost Always | Always |
|---|---|---|---|---|---|
| phone, memos, reports | | | | | |
| • Greeted by name by other employees | 1 | 2 | 3 | 4 | 5 |
| • Given credit for ideas that are adopted | 1 | 2 | 3 | 4 | 5 |
| • Results of work activities significantly impact that of others | 1 | 2 | 3 | 4 | 5 |
| • Opportunity to utilize highest level of skills possessed, at least some of the time | 1 | 2 | 3 | 4 | 5 |
| • Supervisors accurately understand the level of skills | 1 | 2 | 3 | 4 | 5 |

| Characteristic | Never | Rarely | Sometimes | Almost Always | Always |
|---|---|---|---|---|---|
| required for the job | | | | | |
| • Assigned projects of equal importance as peers | 1 | 2 | 3 | 4 | 5 |
| • Opportunity to provide input into important decisions | 1 | 2 | 3 | 4 | 5 |
| • Opportunity for significant participation in performance evaluation | 1 | 2 | 3 | 4 | 5 |
| • Receive frequent feedback on work performance | 1 | 2 | 3 | 4 | 5 |
| • High-level managers aware of results of | 1 | 2 | 3 | 4 | 5 |

| Characteristic | Never | Rarely | Sometimes | Almost Always | Always |
|---|---|---|---|---|---|
| work activities | | | | | |
| • Problems that hinder your performance receive prompt attention from supervisors | 1 | 2 | 3 | 4 | 5 |
| • Opportunities exist for job advancement and/or enhancement | 1 | 2 | 3 | 4 | 5 |
| • Suggestions for improvements receive serious consideration | 1 | 2 | 3 | 4 | 5 |
| • Given credit for ideas that are adopted | 1 | 2 | 3 | 4 | 5 |

| Characteristic | Never | Rarely | Sometimes | Almost Always | Always |
|---|---|---|---|---|---|
| • Praise for good work given in front of other employees | 1 | 2 | 3 | 4 | 5 |
| Other: _____ | 1 | 2 | 3 | 4 | 5 |
| _____ | 1 | 2 | 3 | 4 | 5 |
| _____ | 1 | 2 | 3 | 4 | 5 |

Can you think of other job characteristics that signify recognition to you? Are there some things that you feel are important in conveying recognition? If so, add them to the profile, whether or not they are currently a part of your job.

When you have finished rating the job characteristics, use a straight line to connect the circles indicating your responses to complete your Recognition Profile. If the line jogs to the left of the middle column, your job might be lacking in that recognition characteristic. A jog to the right means that recognition characteristic might be a strength of your job.

While promotions and awards are nice, recognition needs to occur regularly—every day if possible. If we are not visible, we cannot expect people to know who we are. If no one knows our name, we cannot feel unique. If we do not have a chance to communicate with others, we cannot express our individuality and we will not feel recognized.

For example, when Carolyn completed this exercise, she discovered that she wanted a great deal more recognition than she was getting. Her Recognition Profile looked like this.

| *Characteristic* | *Never* | *Rarely* | *Sometimes* | *Almost Always* | *Always* |
|---|---|---|---|---|---|
| • Physically visible to co-workers or public | 1 | ②| 3 | 4 | 5 |
| • Frequent communica-tion with co-workers | 1 | ② | 3 | 4 | 5 |
| • Frequent communica-tion with supervisors | 1 | ② | 3 | 4 | 5 |
| • Frequent communica-tion with other people, e.g., clients | 1 | 2 | ③ | 4 | 5 |
| • Name is used in process of work | 1 | 2 | ③ | 4 | 5 |

## Staying Up When Your Job Pulls You Down

| Characteristic | Never | Rarely | Sometimes | Almost Always | Always |
|---|---|---|---|---|---|
| activities, e.g., on phone, memos, reports | | | | | |
| • Greeted by name by other employees | 1 | ②| 3 | 4 | 5 |
| • Given credit for ideas that are adopted | ① | 2 | 3 | 4 | 5 |
| • Results of work activities significantly impact that of others | 1 | 2 | 3 | ④ | 5 |
| • Opportunity to utilize highest level of skills possessed, at least some of the time | 1 | 2 | 3 | ④ | 5 |
| • Supervisors accurately understand the level of | 1 | 2 | 3 | ④ | 5 |

| Characteristic | Never | Rarely | Sometimes | Almost Always | Always |
|---|---|---|---|---|---|
| skills required for the job | | | | | |
| • Assigned projects of equal importance as peers | 1 | 2 | 3 | ④ | 5 |
| • Opportunity to provide input into important decisions | 1 | 2 | ③ | 4 | 5 |
| • Opportunity for significant participation in performance evaluation | 1 | 2 | 3 | ④ | 5 |
| • Receive frequent feedback on work performance | 1 | ② | 3 | 4 | 5 |
| • High-level managers aware of | 1 | 2 | 3 | ④ | 5 |

| Characteristic | Never | Rarely | Sometimes | Almost Always | Always |
|---|---|---|---|---|---|
| results of work activities | | | | | |
| • Problems that hinder your performance receive prompt attention from supervisors | 1 | 2 | 3 | ④ | 5 |
| • Opportunities exist for job advancement and/or enhancement | 1 | 2 | ③ | 4 | 5 |
| • Suggestions for improvements receive serious consideration | 1 | 2 | 3 | ④ | 5 |
| • Given credit for ideas that are adopted | 1 | 2 | ③ | 4 | 5 |

120

| Characteristic | Never | Rarely | Sometimes | Almost Always | Always |
|---|---|---|---|---|---|
| • Praise for good work given in front of other employees | ①✓ | 2 | 3 | 4 | 5 |
| Other: _____ | 1 | 2 | 3 | 4 | 5 |
| _____ | 1 | 2 | 3 | 4 | 5 |
| _____ | 1 | 2 | 3 | 4 | 5 |

When Carolyn completed her Recognition Profile, she realized that she had considerably a stronger need for recognition than she did for her needs for respect or responsibility. Carolyn rated her job as lacking in the following characteristics.

| Characteristic | Never | Rarely | Sometimes | Almost Always | Always |
|---|---|---|---|---|---|
| • Physically visible to co-workers or public | 1 | ② | 3 | 4 | 5 |
| • Frequent communication with co-workers | 1 | ② | 3 | 4 | 5 |

| Characteristic | Never | Rarely | Sometimes | Almost Always | Always |
|---|---|---|---|---|---|
| • Frequent communication with supervisors | 1 | (2) | 3 | 4 | 5 |
| • Greeted by name by other employees | 1 | (2) | 3 | 4 | 5 |
| • Given credit for ideas that are adopted | (1) | 2 | 3 | 4 | 5 |
| • High-level managers aware of results of work activities | 1 | (2) | 3 | 4 | 5 |
| • Praise for good work given in front of other employees | (1) | 2 | 3 | 4 | 5 |

When Carolyn saw the results of her Recognition Profile, she began to understand why she felt unappreciated. She rarely communicated with her co-workers or the company management except for her immediate supervisor. Other employees did not speak to her when they saw her, and many did not know her name. Finally, even though Carolyn did hear that some of her ideas were adopted by the company, they never were attributed to her.

Carolyn wanted to be acknowledged for her good work; to receive some attention for her innovations. She did not consider other sources of recognition, though. She overlooked the recognition that also comes from being visible to other people in the company, having others greet her by name, and communicating with her co-workers. Yet these were forms of recognition that she could structure herself.

Once Carolyn expanded her understanding of recognition, she began doing many of the very things that would make her more visible and recognizable, such as going to the company cafeteria for lunch. Carolyn had been acting out her frustration with her boss in order to cope, but she was overlooking her own needs in the process. She wasn't getting what she really wanted.

Another client of ours, Lee, is an example of how, through our behaviors, we sometimes hold ourselves back from the very thing we want most.

Lee came for career counseling because he had decided to change jobs. At twenty-five, he was an assistant manager of a company that operated apartments and condominiums, mainly catering to singles. The company maintained several complexes throughout a large metropolitan area. Lee had considerable skills in planning, organization, and public relations, all of which were put to good use in his type of work.

"I don't have any complaints about the work or the firm," Lee began. "In fact, I'd like to stay with the company; the apartment business is going to be really profitable for a while. In fact, the owners are considering opening some complexes in other cities, and there could be some good opportunities. But the owners of the apartment complex live in another city and they don't know what I do. They don't see that the reason we maintain a ninety-five-percent occupancy rate is because of me. I'll never be able to get them to make me a manager. My supervisor, Vivien, favors the other assistant manager, Chris. I'm the one who has developed brochures, posters, publicity parties—things that really get our name out in front of people. I think Chris gets all the credit for our success."

Lee had become entirely focused on his belief that his supervisor was not recognizing his abilities and that she favored Chris, the other assistant manager. In his eyes Chris had become his opponent, someone he needed to outperform in order to get his supervisor's attention. Whether these perceptions were true or not, they consumed Lee's energies; all of his efforts were directed toward these concerns. Let's follow Lee through just two steps of the ADD Strategy.

## Step One: Analyze Your Behaviors

Lee's efforts to explore his early memories revealed that there were some events from his childhood that explained why certain types of recognition needs were so strong. Lee had grown up with three brothers, all of whom were at least ten years older than he was. Lee was the baby. The entire family delighted in pampering him.

Lee's father managed a manufacturing business that his own father had started. All of his life Lee had heard his father say that he was looking forward to the day when his sons would run the business. Each of the boys had left college after two years and had automatically taken their places in the business. When Lee was in college, however, his father and brothers were upset when Lee wanted to quit school and go to work with them.

"You're going to be the one to finish," they told him. "There's absolutely no reason for you to be here. We want you to get that degree."

As a result, it seemed Lee was out to prove something—if not to his father and brothers, then certainly to himself. He had decided not to go into the family business after all, feeling that he needed to make it on his own instead.

Lee had transferred his need for approval to his current situation. Instead of his father, he tried to get Vivien's attention. Instead of his brothers, he vied with Chris for recognition.

With the help of a friend, Lee analyzed his behaviors to determine which ones were acting out his frustrations rather than helping solve the problem. It took Lee several tries to be totally honest with himself and get to the heart of the matter.

Lee admitted that he had delayed giving Chris phone messages and had withheld information from her that might have helped her do her work. He had begun shouting at the maintenance workers at the complex and had come close to doing the same with several delivery persons.

Additionally, Lee had complained to his supervisor about Chris, attempting to prove that he was more productive than she was. Finally Lee had bottled up his angry feelings so much that he had exploded several times, slamming objects around in the office.

When Lee reviewed the acting-out behaviors he had identified, he remarked that it was obvious he was a person who was not used to being second. Instead, he had been the center of attention in his family, and he still craved this recognition.

Lee completed an exercise to examine the types of recognition he had been receiving.

The types of recognition people usually receive were listed in the left-hand column of the form Lee completed. Lee indicated whether each was a type of recognition he had been receiving or whether it was one he didn't have but wanted. Next he indicated the source of the recognition. The following are Lee's answers.

| Type of Recognition | Have? | Want? | Source |
|---|---|---|---|
| Raise | x | | Supervisor |
| Promotion | | x | Apartment Owners |

| Type of Recognition | Have? | Want? | Source |
|---|---|---|---|
| New title | | x | Apartment Owners |
| Written praise | x | | Supervisor |
| Verbal praise | x | | Supervisor |
| Memos | x | | Co-workers & Supervisor |
| Phone calls | x | | Co-workers & Supervisor |
| Other: | | | |
| Good ratings on activity evaluations | x | | Tenants |

Lee's answers indicated that he was receiving recognition, but not from the people he really wanted to recognize him. He had received raises from his superior, as well as written and verbal praise. He had a great deal of interaction with employees at his own company as well as those from other companies that did business with the apartments. Also, the tenants always gave him good feedback on the activities he organized.

While it was nice that Lee's boss, co-workers, and tenants recognized his achievements, the owners were the people he really wanted to impress. Yet his behaviors up until now were aimed at his supervisor and the other assistant manager. Instead Lee needed to target his efforts toward the owners of the apartment complexes.

Eventually Lee was able to see that his repeated attempts to change Vivien, his supervisor, had been acting-out behaviors. It almost seemed, in fact, that Lee had lost sight of his goal—to get the owners to make him a manager of one of their new operations. Instead his efforts had focused on getting Vivien to approve of him more than she approved of Chris.

### Step Two: Determine What You Really Want

Like Lee, many of us have the tendency to become so focused on a job problem that we overlook an obvious solution. We are caught up in the unfairness, the absurdity, or the incongruity of the situation. These incongruities come to shape our behaviors even though they do not solve the problem. We lose sight of what we really want. As Lee did, we need to focus on our recognition needs instead.

When Lee completed his Recognition Profile, he discovered that there were several signs of recognition in his job. He was highly visible, he communicated with others frequently, and he had the opportunity to use his skills.

Lee's profile indicated, though, that the owners were not aware of his good work. Also, although there were opportunities for job advancement, Lee noted that he was not sure whether he would be considered for these.

Next, in order to guide Lee in identifying what he really wanted, he listed his acting-out behaviors and described how these behaviors were sabotaging his recognition needs. His list looked like this.

| Acting-Out Behavior | How This Sabotages My Recognition |
|---|---|
| 1. Withhold information that would help Chris | 1. I eventually will make an enemy of her |
| 2. Delay giving Chris phone messages | 2. I could expect her to do the same to me |
| 3. Ignore my angry feelings | 3. Causes me to explode |
| 4. Shout at maintenance workers at the complex | 4. Brings *negative* attention |
| 5. Complain to Vivien | 5. Makes her think worse of me |
| 6. Slam things around the office | 6. Childish reaction |

Lee's acting-out behaviors of complaining, slamming things, and shouting at people were childish reactions that eventually would bring him attention, but it would be negative attention. Also, complaining to Vivien without constructively trying to solve the problem made him look like a whiner.

Lee eventually developed an action plan that allowed him to put his job problems in the proper perspective. He began writing down his projects, keeping a record of how the activity had been promoted and what the results were. In this way he developed a portfolio of his accomplishments that he could present to the owners when they were in town. This allowed Lee to remain focused on the recognition he really wanted.

## Your Turn

How about you? What did the analysis of your behaviors reveal? Do your behaviors bring you the kind of attention you want? Or is there something else that you could be doing to have others notice you as you want to be noticed? What kinds of feedback have you received about your behaviors?

In order to become more aware of your own need for recognition and its importance in your job, complete the same exercise that Lee did. Be honest with yourself in identifying the types of recognition you receive and the types you want. Indicate the source of each type of recognition so that you can see if you are targeting the right people. In the spaces marked "Other," write in any types of recognition that are not already listed on the form.

| *Type of Recognition* | *Have?* | *Want?* | *Source* |
| --- | --- | --- | --- |
| Raise | | | |
| Promotion | | | |
| New title | | | |
| Written praise | | | |
| Verbal praise | | | |
| Awards | | | |
| Memos | | | |
| Phone calls | | | |
| Written praise | | | |
| Other: | | | |

Do your responses indicate that you are being recognized by the groups that are important to you? Are you focusing your efforts on the right people? If you had trouble thinking of answers, keep track for several days of the recognition you receive and then come back to this exercise.

Now describe how your acting-out behaviors might be sabotaging your sense of recognition and keeping you from getting what you really want.

| *Description of Acting-Out Behavior* | *How This Sabotages My Recognition* |
|---|---|
| 1. _____ | 1. _____ |
| 2. _____ | 2. _____ |
| 3. _____ | 3. _____ |
| 4. _____ | 4. _____ |
| 5. _____ | 5. _____ |

Being recognized does not require us to achieve great things or to have a high-level work position. We can be surrounded every day by people who recognize us if we make the effort to reach out to others. We need only to develop relationships with others, to reframe our picture of recognition, and to affirm the recognition that we already have.

Using the ADD Strategy, we can help ourselves learn how to increase our sense of recognition. We can learn to analyze our behaviors, pinpoint sabotaging behaviors, and determine what we really want.

Up to this point we have Analyzed our behaviors and have Determined what it is we really want. Next, we will address the third and final step in the ADD Strategy. This last step is about learning to Develop an action plan that will help you to receive, replenish, and retain the Basic Three Rs for a more positive self-concept. This is the step that will ADD the ability to stay up when the job pulls you down.

# CHAPTER 8

## Step Three—
## Developing a
## Plan of Action

SO FAR WE have worked through steps one and two of the ADD Strategy, a strategy designed to help us stay up during pulling-down times. Now we will briefly review steps one and two, using Tonya as our example. Finally we will continue into step three: Developing an Action Plan, again using Tonya to illustrate how it works. Thus we will follow her through the entire ADD Strategy.

To refresh your memory, Tonya was the person who needed to consult with the president of her social service agency's board of directors prior to their monthly board meeting. She had interpreted the board president's actions as being a sign that he did not respect her or recognize her contributions to the organization. She became so focused on the problem that she developed some very counterproductive acting-out behaviors in order to cope with her frustration.

In Step One, ANALYZE YOUR BEHAVIORS when your job pulls you down, Tonya identified behaviors that were counterproductive. She discovered that some of her acting-out behaviors began long ago, when she was a child. "It seems like I've always gotten stuck when something is bothering me," she said. "I sort of spin my wheels without accomplishing anything."

Tonya acknowledged that her own acting-out behaviors might be keeping her from getting what she really wanted. By complaining, wasting time, and becoming edgy, Tonya was resorting to behaviors that sabotaged her ability to fulfill her need for more of a sense of Respect, Responsibility, and Recognition.

With the help of a co-worker Tonya noted these acting-out behaviors: (1) complain to anyone who will listen, (2) waste time stewing about it, and (3) get edgy about the upcoming board meeting.

In Step Two, DETERMINE WHAT YOU REALLY WANT, we had Tonya complete profiles of her Basic Three-R needs to help her determine what she really wanted. Her profiles indicated that her job met many aspects of her Three-R needs in some ways but not in others. She especially wanted the president to recognize and respect her contribution to the company's mission.

At this point we will now bring Tonya to the final step of the ADD Strategy, which is DEVELOPING AN ACTION PLAN.

The purpose of step three of the ADD Strategy is to develop an action plan to develop behaviors to stay up during pulling-down times. This action plan will enable us to replace acting-out behaviors with staying-up behaviors. Staying-up behaviors help us to meet our Basic Three-R needs, resulting in more positive feelings about ourselves and our job.

As we develop an action plan, we will do three things.

- We will make a list of the acting-out behaviors we identified in step one;
- We will replace each acting-out behavior with a staying-up behavior;
- We will outline specific steps to ensure our plan's success.

## TONYA

When Tonya followed this action-planning procedure, she first made a list of her acting-out behaviors:

### TONYA'S ACTION PLAN

I. Acting-Out Behaviors
  1. Complain to anyone who will listen
  2. Waste time stewing about it
  3. Get edgy about next month's meeting

## TONYA'S ACTION PLAN (*cont.*)

II. Next Tonya replaced each acting-out behavior with a staying-up behavior.

| *Acting-Out Behaviors* | *Staying-Up Behaviors* |
|---|---|
| 1. Complain to anyone who will listen | 1. Talk to only one person about it |
| 2. Waste time stewing about it | 2. Do something I need to do while I'm stewing about it |
| 3. Get edgy about next month's meeting | 3. Prepare a few items a month early |

III. Finally Tonya outlined a step-by-step plan to make sure she followed through.

| *Staying-Up Behavior* | *Action Steps* |
|---|---|
| 1. Talk to Cindy about the problem | 1. *Ask Cindy* if she will be my "comfort" person |
| | 2. *Call Cindy* for lunch on the day I start calling the president |
| | 3. *Give myself 5 minutes* to complain at lunch |
| | 4. *Limit* any complaint calls to Cindy to 5 minutes |

| *Staying-Up Behavior* | *Action Steps* |
|---|---|
| 2. Do something I need to do while I'm stewing about it | 1. *Collect all the floppy discs* I need to reorganize, copy, etc. |
| | 2. *Arrange them* together next to my computer |
| | 3. *Work on them* whenever I find myself unable to stop stewing about the situation |
| 3. Try to prepare a few things for the next meeting a month early | 1. *Make a list* of next month's agenda items I need to talk to the president about |
| | 2. *Write a summary paragraph* about each one |
| | 3. *Show the president* the summaries at this month's meeting |
| | 4. *Ask him* what I can be working on now—to help him better prepare for the next meeting, too |

Tonya knew that this new strategy of responding to pulling-down times would not always be easy, so she left herself no room to slip back into her old acting-out behaviors. Notice how specific she was in replacing her acting-out behaviors with staying-up ones. By planning out each action step, Tonya ensured her success in changing her behaviors.

Tonya knew that these staying-up behaviors would help her feel a greater sense of control over meeting her needs for Respect, Responsibility, and Recognition. Thus Tonya acknowledged that meaningingful change must first start with her. Ultimately, she cultivated the attitude and skills needed to stay up during pulling-down times by using a well-planned strategy.

Let's look now at Stephanie and Judy, two examples of people who also learned to develop staying-up behaviors. Stephanie was the manager of the direct-mail operations for her company, a market research organization. She liked having responsibility, but she felt that her boss dumped too much work on her, and she did not always feel confident of her ability to handle the assignments.

Judy also had a problem with her sense of responsibility in her job as office manager for the credit department of a large bank. Judy wanted *more* responsibility. Judy's new boss would give her very explicit instructions on how to perform even the simplest duties, and Judy concluded that her boss did not like her or trust her.

Here are the action plans Stephanie and Judy developed.

## STEPHANIE

Stephanie began taking pressure off her boss by relying more on her own judgment. This allowed her to feel good about herself. Here are her responses to the action-planning procedure.

### STEPHANIE'S ACTION PLAN

I. Acting-Out Behaviors
  1. Ask my boss for approval on every detail of a project
  2. Question new ideas
  3. Perform tasks in the same way all the time
  4. Dwell on the negative

II. *Acting-Out Behaviors*

  1. Ask my boss for approval on every detail
  2. Question new ideas
  3. Perform tasks in the same way
  4. Dwell on the negative

*Staying-Up Behaviors*

  1. Rely on my own judgment more
  2. Remain open to new ideas
  3. Experiment with new methods
  4. Focus on the positive

## STEPHANIE'S ACTION PLAN (*cont.*)

| *Staying-Up Behavior* | *Action Steps* |
| --- | --- |
| 1. Rely more on my own judgment | 1. *Organize my ideas* when my boss gives me an assignment<br>2. *Write an outline* of my ideas<br>3. *Go with* the best decision I can make at the time |
| 2. Remain open to new ideas | 1. *Keep quiet* when I hear a new idea<br>2. *Think about the idea* when I'm alone<br>3. *Write down my questions* as I'm thinking<br>4. *Develop positive ways* of asking my questions |
| 3. Try some new methods | 1. *Put a suggestion box* by the coffeepot for my staff<br>2. *Discuss one suggestion* at each staff meeting<br>3. *Implement new methods* that seem workable |

| *Staying-Up Behavior* | *Action Steps* |
|---|---|
| 4. Focus on the positive | 1. *Make a list* each day of the good things that happened |
| | 2. *Share them with a co-worker* |

## JUDY

When Judy stood back and took an honest look at her situation, she admitted that she had not initiated responsibility as she should have. She probably had given her new supervisor the impression that she was not a responsible person.

Judy discovered that she was not following up on projects or office procedures, both of which were in her job description. Additionally, she had allowed her job problems to affect the other parts of her life. Judy identified staying-up behaviors to replace the acting-out behaviors. Then she developed action steps that looked like this.

### JUDY'S ACTION PLAN

| *Staying-Up Behaviors* | *Action Steps* |
|---|---|
| 1. Initiate projects that need to be done | 1. *Requisition an electronic calendar software program* for my computer |
| | 2. *Mark the due dates* for 20 routine projects in progress, e.g., data entry, expense reports |

141

## JUDY'S ACTION PLAN (*cont.*)

| *Staying-Up Behaviors* | *Action Steps* |
|---|---|
| | 3. *Indicate starting dates* for new projects |
| | 4. *Put a reminder note* one week before each is due |
| | 5. *Print the calendar* for my boss the first of each month |
| 2. Keep my job problems in perspective | 1. *List my goals*, e.g., put daughter through college, save for retirement |
| | 2. *Rank them* in order of priority |
| 3. Keep track of the projects I distribute to the office staff and report the office procedures that need to be changed | 1. *Get in touch with Dave* in computing about developing a tracking program for office procedures |
| | 2. *Record projects* in one file and office procedures in another |

| *Staying-Up Behaviors* | *Action Steps* |
|---|---|
| | 3. *Enter notes daily* on progress of projects and procedures that aren't working right, e.g., taking too long to enter data in mornings, change to three times a day |
| | 4. *Compile notes* into a report and *submit to my boss* weekly |
| 4. Come to work unless I'm really sick | 1. *Pick out something* I really want, e.g., clothes, magazine, compact disc |
| | 2. *Buy it* for myself if I make it to work all day when I've thought about staying home |
| 5. Learn some new software programs | 1. *Call community college* for class bulletin |
| | 2. *Check with training department* for ideas |
| | 3. *Enroll in a class* by fall |

143

Like Stephanie, Judy had taken a bad situation and looked honestly at herself and her own reactions.

## STAN

Stan was another person who showed us how he learned to meet his own Basic Three-R needs. Stan was the 52-year-old ex-executive who had opted to take a demotion rather than an early retirement when his company reorganized. He did not mind his new job, and in fact he rather enjoyed being able to use the accounting skills he had developed in previous years. But Stan did miss the certain kind of recognition that he had enjoyed as a leader.

Since Stan could not use all of his leadership skills in his current job, he developed an action plan to utilize them in a professional association. He also decided to run for the board of trustees of the local community college. Also, in the past, Stan had been actively involved in youth ministry at his church until his hectic schedule had prevented such an involvement. Lately he had been considering serving as a mentor to youth at his local church. Stan's action plan looked like this.

## STAN'S ACTION PLAN

I. Acting-Out Behaviors
  1. Withdrawing my help from others
  2. Not using my leadership skills

| II. *Acting-Out Behaviors* | *Staying-Up Behaviors* |
|---|---|
| 1. Withdrawing my help from others | 1. Offer to help others |
| 2. Not using my leadership skills | 2. Become active as a leader in the community |

| III. *Staying-Up Behavior* | *Action Steps* |
|---|---|
| 1. Offer to help others at work and outside of work | 1. *Teach* Carrie Lotus 1-2-3 at work<br>2. *Become mentor* for youth group at church |
| 2. Become active as a leader in the community | 1. *Run for office* to be on local college board of trustees<br>2. *Join* a professional association<br>3. *Join* Kiwanis Club |

## CAROLYN

Like Stan, Carolyn, the administrative assistant, developed an action plan to meet her Basic Three-R needs with Staying-Up behaviors. Carolyn was not sure exactly why she was being overlooked for a promotion. She had only a vague feeling that her boss might be taking credit for her ideas. Carolyn in fact might never know what the exact barrier was, and the more she dwelt on it, the more frustrated she became.

In step three of the ADD Strategy, Carolyn decided that she needed to focus on her goal of a promotion rather than becoming sidetracked by a situation with her boss that might or might not have been the real barrier. When she chose to concentrate on her own future, she was able to rise above present job problems.

Let's follow Carolyn through the action planning procedure, as she listed her acting-out behaviors, replaced them with staying-up behaviors, and outlined action steps.

### CAROLYN'S ACTION PLAN

I. Acting-Out Behaviors
  1. Sulk and stay in office
  2. Neglect some responsibilities
  3. Eat alone
  4. Act impatiently with my own staff

II. *Acting-Out Behaviors*

1. Sulk and stay in office
2. Neglect some responsibilities
3. Eat alone

4. Act impatiently with my own staff

*Staying-Up Behaviors*

1. Get out and around—be visible and network
2. Pay attention to all responsibilities
3. Eat with Karen, Dave, or other co-workers
4. Listen carefully and respond to my staff

III. *Staying-Up Behavior*

1. Get out and around—be visible

2. Pay attention to all responsibilities

*Action Steps*

1. *Give* myself a pep talk
2. *Get up* out of my chair
3. *March* to the door
4. *Head* for the hallway
5. *Smile* and *say hello* to people
6. *Stop and describe* my latest projects

1. *Make a list* of the things I'm neglecting
2. Schedule them on my calendar every week

147

CAROLYN'S ACTION PLAN (*cont.*)

| *Staying-Up Behavior* | *Action Steps* |
|---|---|
| | 3. Cross them out when completed |
| 3. Eat with co-workers and get to know them. | 1. *Go to company cafeteria* for lunch at least twice a week |
| | 2. *Sit* with new people |
| | 3. *Introduce* myself |
| | 4. *Ask other people* about themselves |
| | 5. *Talk* about my work |
| 4. Listen carefully and respond to my staff | 1. *Excuse* myself when I become impatient |
| | 2. *Go* to my office |
| | 3. *Repeat* to myself this message: It is not this person's fault that I have not gotten a promotion. If I jump on this person for no reason, I will only be making things worse for myself. |
| | 4. *Go back* and *start* a conversation with the person |
| | 5. *Praise* the person for at least one thing |

This plan worked for Carolyn. She developed actions and attitudes that would lead to a promotion in the future. If she did decide to change jobs eventually, it would be a planned career move, not one of desperation. In the meantime she was able to take control of her own needs and restore a positive self-concept.

Like the people in these examples, we might act out when we have job conflicts and frustrations. Instead we can use the ADD Strategy as a step-by-step method for responding with staying-up behaviors when there is a specific job problem or a sense of mundaneness about our jobs.

**Your Turn**

Now try making your action plan. To get ready, think back to steps one and two of the ADD Strategy. What acting-out behaviors did you identify in a specific pulling-down situation? What aspects of any of the Basic Three Rs did you decide you really want?

Finally, follow the action-planning procedure the people in our examples used. List the acting-out behaviors you identified and replace each one with a staying-up behavior that meets your Basic Three-R needs and helps you feel good about yourself. Then develop an action plan with specific steps for developing each Staying-Up behavior.

I. *Acting-Out Behaviors*

    1.

    2.

    3.

    4.

II. *Acting-Out Behaviors*      *Staying-Up Behaviors*

    1.                  1.

    2.                  2.

    3.                  3.

    4.                  4.

## ACTION PLAN

III. *Staying-Up Behaviors*      *Action Steps*

    1.                  1.
                           2.
                           3.
                           4.

III. *Staying-Up Behaviors*  *Action Steps*

    2.               1.
                        2.
                        3.
                        4.

    3.               1.
                        2.
                        3.
                        4.

    4.               1.
                        2.
                        3.
                        4.

## Pointers for Successful Action Plans

As you polish your plan, here are some final pointers you should keep in mind.

1. *Be Totally Honest*

   Often, we tend to protect our feelings by seeing only what others are doing *to* us rather than recognizing our own responses and contributions to a job conflict.

   Carolyn felt much more comfortable saying to herself, "I'm getting a rotten deal because they won't promote me," than she did saying, "I really do tend to react by staying in my office more than I should."

We need to step back and take a long, honest look at our behaviors in order to develop an effective action plan.

2. *Keep It Simple*

Sometimes the most effective solution to our problems might be the most simple.

Judy conjured up all kinds of reasons why she wasn't given more responsibility—her supervisor did not like her, she did not really have very good skills, and so on. Finally Judy realized that she merely needed to initiate more responsibilities herself; her supervisor probably was waiting for her to take responsibility.

Like Judy, our tendency often is to make solutions more complicated than they need to be. When it comes to action plans, though, we should follow the old KISS technique: Keep It Simple and Straightforward.

3. *Make It Specific*

In order to stay up when our job pulls us down, we need to know exactly what we can do and how we should act.

What if Judy had said to herself, "I am going to start taking more responsibility"? Would she have done it? Possibly not; at least not consistently. Instead, by specifying exactly how she would organize projects and propose them to her supervisor, she was not leaving anything to chance.

One way to fill in the details for a specific action

plan is to ask yourself questions such as: "*What* exactly will I do?" or "*How* will I do it?"

4. *Make It Positive*

Notice the difference between the statements in each of these sets:

#1 A. "I will not eat lunch alone anymore."

　　B. "I will eat and network with other people."

#2 A. "I won't become impatient and cutting with my staff."

　　B. "I will begin giving more open and constructive criticism and honest feedback to my staff.

Statement A in each set is a negative version of statement B; it says much the same thing but with a different emphasis.

Psychologically, we all receive more of a boost from positive statements such as "I will" or "I can" than we do from negative statements like "I won't" or "I can't."

5. *Keep It Realistic*

Tonya knew that she needed to blow off steam to someone when the board president delayed their meetings. If she had tried to keep her anger to herself, she would not have succeeded. Tonya thought it *was* possible, though, for her to talk to only one person about it and to limit the time that she complained. This was a more realistic goal.

By asking ourselves, "Is this action within my

153

control?" we can set ourselves up for success instead of failure.

6. *Write It Down*

A written action plan will give us more of a commitment to changing our acting-out behaviors into staying-up behaviors. It's too easy to go back on our good intentions and tell ourselves, "Oh, well. It really doesn't matter." Having them written down, within our easy sight, reinforces our commitment to our plans.

7. *Keep at It*

Stephanie wrote an action plan to become more open and accepting of new ideas. She found that the first twenty-one days were the most difficult. It was not always easy. Sometimes she felt that she was taking two steps forward and one step back. However, she had made a conscious commitment to keep at it. Eventually she found it easier to remember to react with staying-up behaviors instead of acting-out behaviors.

8. *Evaluate and Revise Your Action Plan*

"How can I know if my action plan is a good one?" is a question we often hear. We always tell our clients that if it works, don't fix it!

Ask yourself these questions. Is the problem getting better? Do I view myself with more Respect, Responsibility, and Recognition? If your answer to either of these questions is yes, your action plan is working. If your answer is no, you need to revise it.

Originally, when Tonya chose to find a comfort buddy to complain to, she found herself complaining for such a long time that she only became more upset. So she revised her plan to limit her complaint time to five minutes. It worked for her.

9. *Give Yourself a Reward*
Rewards are an effective means of motivation. Judy was able to overcome her tendency to call in sick by rewarding herself when she disciplined herself to go to work. "I really felt silly at first," Judy shared with us. "But it worked, and that was what really mattered."

10. *Keep a Record and Share Your Success Stories*
Judy kept a floppy disc with her calendar of projects and her weekly reports to her supervisor. After one month she could print out her file and feel a real sense of accomplishment. She shared her method of organization with a co-worker who was having trouble staying organized.

"I was really surprised at how much I had done," Judy told us. "I also felt good that I helped someone else get a better grip on her work, too."

Like Judy, we can build a system into our action plans for recording our progress, whether it is keeping a file on a disc, writing in a journal, or jotting notes on our calendar. Also, we can make it a point to share our successes with others.

155

Remember that the main purpose of an action plan is to cultivate staying-up behaviors that make us feel good about ourselves during pulling-down times. It is a systematic approach to problem-solving that enables us to choose the best approach to address a problem with three simple steps: (1) by listing acting-out behaviors, (2) by replacing acting-out behaviors with staying-up (or productive) behaviors, and (3) by planning steps to ensure their implementation.

After using the ADD Strategy for a while, it will become automatic and we will find ourselves routinely changing acting-out behaviors into staying-up behaviors that meet our Basic Three-R needs during pulling-down times.

# CHAPTER 9

## Adding It All Up

IT SEEMS ONLY logical that we should take control of our own job satisfaction. Self-control is all we truly have. People everywhere are demanding a voice in what happens to them, searching for control in all areas of their lives. Self-control, self-determination, and self-fulfillment are the cries of the 1990s, cries that promise to swell to a roar as we move toward the twenty-first century.

In the midst of these trends toward self-control, self-determination, and self-fulfillment, however, are equally potent forces that sometimes cause us to feel out-of-control, other-determined, and unfulfilled. As managers hint of possible layoffs, our imaginations picture the CEO and vice-presidents spinning a giant wheel of fortune to produce the employee numbers of the people who will be discharged. We sometimes feel about as much in control of our careers as an automobile with no steering mechanism.

Is there any good news in this paradox? Yes! There is good news for people who are listening. The good news is that the job-satisfaction myths are crumbling. They began eroding slowly toward the end of the 1980s and now they are beginning to tumble.

Employees are deciding that a linear vault to the board-room is not the only criterion of career success. As people in the workplace discover that it is difficult to have it all, they are asking, "Who really wants it at that price, anyway?" Businesses, in turn, are developing dual-track career paths and other innovative incentives for workers who reject the management-is-where-it's-at hype.

We are liberated when we realize that we do not have to ask for anyone's permission before we tailor our career goals to fit our own specific situations. It means that if we would rather spend our weekends playing the violin in a community orchestra than attend business-related social events in order to rub elbows with the brass, this is our decision, no one else's. If that decision also means that we need to cancel the celebration we were planning for our next promotion, that is okay too; it is, after all, our own decision and under our own control.

How we decide to interpret what happens to us is the crux of a feeling of control. These daily decisions in turn become the bedrock of our job satisfaction. Reframing a viewpoint, finding a different way, creating alternatives—these are the career tools of the future for those who are determined to find satisfaction.

Our traditional idea of authority and our childhood lessons in helplessness are being rewritten, and we are the authors. We can write a leading role for ourselves in which we come out the winner, the person who finishes first.

## Job-Satisfaction Myths

Sometimes our definition of job satisfaction may sound good philosophically, but in reality may need reworking. We often believe myths about our jobs. Have you believed any of the following?

**Myth #1.** *There is a perfect job for me.*
There is no perfect job. Jobs have descriptions, but we each bring definition and meaning to our job. The job is in the process of being perfected only as we fulfill our intrinsic job needs, which are our sense of Respect, Responsibility, and Recognition.

**Myth #2.** *Some jobs are more important than others.*
If as human beings we are important—and we are—then the job is important because we impart of ourselves into the job. Status is only in the mind of the thinker. People who care about themselves and care about their work realize that no one can do their job like they can. The job is special because they are special. There is dignity and self-respect that is imparted to the job.

159

**Myth #3.** *I must make myself fit the job.*

Individuals who accept themselves and their self-worth tend naturally to be creative problem-solvers. They tend to look for ways to make situations and circumstances work in their favor. In other words, when they are given lemons they find ways to make lemonade. They make the job work for them rather than trying to fit the job.

**Myth #4.** *Jobs should have meaning and purpose.*

Jobs have meaning and purpose only to the extent that we give them meaning and purpose. Just as we define our own job satisfaction, we define the meaning and purpose of the job. This starts with knowing our deep values, beliefs, and purpose for living. As we get "the big picture" of these elements of our lives, we can begin putting our job in perspective within a larger picture. This will also help us make the job work for us rather than us working for the job.

**Myth #5.** *A job should help me feel better about myself and raise my self-esteem.*

A job will never put something inside you that you don't already have. A job can embellish and strengthen what you have, but never give it to you. It wasn't designed to do that. The better you feel about yourself, the more you will see or create opportunities to maintain these feelings about yourself—even when circumstances try to pull you down.

**Myth #6.** *A job should provide challenge.*
Only to the extent that we begin to look for challenge in our job. We must create our opportunities to be challenged, especially after we have settled in our job and begin feeling secure and competent about how we perform our day-to-day responsibilities.

**Myth #7.** *It's hard to work for a difficult boss.*
The work is not hard. The interpersonal relationship with your boss is what is hard. This strained relationship causes emotional tensions that can be wearing. When we are working for difficult people, it will help if we distinguish between the work and the difficult person. This requires a sense of confidence and competency in ourselves that can keep us centered during trying times.

**Myth #8.** *You may be stuck doing a job for the rest of your working life.*
In the age we are living in, that is highly unlikely. Organizations and corporations are going through massive changes with amazing rapidity. While you might be working for the same company if you choose, the nature and the skill level of that job will likely change as the organization changes.

**Myth #9.** *I must be outstanding on my job.*
Our work may not directly showcase our skills and abilities. That should be okay. The requirement is that you do the best you can with your job assignments.

161

Look for other opportunities in your workplace, perhaps outside of your regular type of responsibility, to let your talents and skills glow.

**Myth #10.** *I should be further along in my job than I am now.* If "further along" means more promotions and salary increases, the truth of the matter is that few of us are getting many of those to any substantial degree. Employees are staying longer in the same position. Salary increases are not as large and frequent as they might have been in the past. It is not fair to ourselves to measure our sense of worth and value by our job titles and the size of income we earn. Our definition of job satisfaction must be a definition that is within our control and can be within our reach. Carefully looking at our personal needs and longings can help us dispel any unrealistic myths we may have about job satisfaction.

## A Truth About Our Jobs

Effectively dealing with pulling-down situations that result in job frustrations and disappointments requires us to start by looking hard within ourselves. This requires honesty about how we see ourselves and what we really want. One simple truth can help us get to this point of honesty so that we can begin to stay up when our job pulls us down: *Each of us defines our own job satisfaction, and each of us must be responsible for our job satisfaction as we define it.*

We can't expect our employer to make us happy. Thus, exploring our definition of job satisfaction becomes central to how we feel about it. And we can be as miserable or as happy about our job situation, whatever it might be, as we choose.

## The ADD Strategy Revisited

The ADD Strategy forces us to stop focusing on people and events we cannot control and instead begin focusing on ourselves. In this way we reframe the way we see ourselves and our situation. By analyzing our own behaviors, we concentrate on the only behaviors we can change—our own. By determining what we really want, we target the person we can influence most—ourselves. By developing an action plan, we prescribe success for an important person's benefit—ours!

Just think of what we could accomplish if we could collect all the energy we have expended on counterproductive reactions to job problems and concentrate this same energy into productive behaviors instead! Imagine the satisfaction we could acquire if we could reframe our thinking to accept the achievement of the Basic Three Rs as being legitimate, serious career goals. The possibilities for personal development would be limitless!

## Making Meaning in Your Work

Terms such as "life enrichment," "inner fulfillment," and "personal goals" have seeped into the workplace and they show no sign of receding. How do these words affect us? Simply put, our definition of job satisfaction can include our own personal development or growth. More importantly, it allows us to bring our own meaning to our work.

The meaning we create in our work is based on our own reactions to events and situations. For some of us, our meaning is the attention we create with our complaints, our criticisms, and our self-described sufferings. Others of us move beyond these traps and understand that real satisfaction comes from behaving in ways that allow us to view ourselves with respect and with the recognition of our own unique responsibility—whatever it might be.

How about you? What meaning do you bring to your work? Are you adding to your life satisfaction by using your job as an important opportunity for personal as well as career development? Do your behaviors allow you to picture yourself through a filter of Respect, Responsibility, and Recognition?

## Staying Up With the Basic Three Rs

The following are proven methods of staying up when your job gets you down. Each is guaranteed to add the Basic Three Rs to your self-concept.

1. *Network*
   Networking has become a buzz word among the career conscious—and for good reason. There is

no better way to create a support group, stay visible, or receive information. Networking is a win-win technique. You not only meet other people, but they meet you, and what better way can there be for staying up when your job pulls you down?

2. *Find a mentor—or become one!*
Having a role model, getting to know people, developing leadership skills—these are just some of the advantages of mentoring. All of us learn from watching other people, observing what they do and what they say. Mentoring is an age-old method of teaching and learning, another technique where everybody wins.

3. *Upgrade your skills or learn some new ones*
Any kind of education or training is like a secret that is tucked away in the back of our minds; it is always there and it can never be taken away from us. Nothing gives us more self-confidence than learning to do something new or in a different way. Perhaps it is something we have always wanted to do but never had the chance. Or it might be something we never thought we could do. Even brushing up on an old skill helps us to know that we can make a valuable contribution.

4. *Get organized!*
In times of stress, we often tend to become depressed, which can make us lethargic, which

leads to more depression, which adds to our lethargy, which—well, you get the picture. In order to avoid the cycle, we sometimes need to force ourselves to become and stay organized. Once we do this, we are empowered by a feeling of control that we did not have before or that we did not think was possible. Organization—it is worth the effort!

5. *Look at your priorities*

What do you value most? Your job? Your family? Do you have specific goals? Are you working to put your kids through college? To buy a new house? To move up the career ladder? Whatever is important to you—that is where your efforts should be directed. Often our job problems are like being on a roller coaster; we hang on for dear life while the train takes us up, down, and around curves, wherever the tracks happen to be going. Instead, we need to focus on our own priorities, engineering the train along the tracks that lead to our destination.

6. *Be around positive people*

We are known by the company we keep. That is an old saying, and perhaps a trite one, but it is true. When we are having problems in our job, why would we want to be around people who pull us down even more? And yet many of us do just that. One of the best ways of staying up when our job pulls us down is to be around people who lift us higher and then support us once we get there.

7. *Look outside of work*

   What if you have tried looking at your job from every conceivable angle and finally have to admit that you are stuck, at least for the time being, in a job that is going nowhere, that does not make you happy, and that probably is not going to change? Should you roll over and give up? Not by any means! There is more than one way of nourishing your self-concept! What about your personal life? Join a club, or better yet, run for a club office. Volunteer your time or take up a hobby. Eat right, exercise, and stay fit. These are good ways of replenishing your Basic Three Rs and reframing the way you see yourself.

8. *Have some humor*

   It is easy to get caught up in our job problems, to take ourselves too seriously, and to lose our perspective on our work life. It helps to step back and pretend that we are watching a situation comedy on television. The characters all act in predictable ways and say predictable things. Lucy gets herself into a mess; Ricky becomes furious with her. Theo brings home a bad report card; the Huxtables lecture him on the merits of education. What about your own life? Are you able to see the humor in your situation? If not, can you rewrite the script to include some laughs?

9. *Count your blessings*

We have heard that we can always find someone with more problems than we have if we look hard enough. Hearing the expression, though, is easier than practicing it. When we actually sit down and list the things that are right in our job, we often are surprised. "But," we might say to ourselves in our more honest moments, "it is rather nice to feel sorry for myself!" That may be true for now, but in the long run, focusing on the positive will help us to stay up, whereas focusing on the negative will only pull us down.

10. *Give of yourself*

There is a reason this is the last tried-and-true staying-up behavior; the reason is that it is the best one. Call it giving of ourselves, call it doing unto others, or call it by any number of other names. They all boil down to the same thing—we cannot expect to be treated with Respect, Responsibility, or Recognition unless we first treat other people that way.

### The Bottom Line

Whatever the job dissatisfaction we are expeiencing, dealing effectively with the problem requires us to deal with ourselves first. With practice we can learn to analyze the problem and its root source. We can be honest and accepting of ourselves and we can ask ourselves what it is we really want from our job. Then we can begin to deal effectively with the problem. We do this by working up a systematic plan of action that ensures that we use staying-up behaviors that will get us what we really want.

Your sense of job satisfaction is like a balance sheet that is waiting to be tabulated. If you subtract when you should add, the total will be wrong, and you might find yourself coming up short—in the red. If you figure the basics correctly, however, the bottom-line total will add up to a profit and the check will be made out to you. So make your first decision now, and add the basics carefully. The answer, after all, is up to you.

# About the Authors

JOANNE BODNER, Ed.D., teaches Career/Life Planning courses at Johnson County Community College, ranked one of the top ten community colleges in the country. She received her professional training at the University of Kansas, where she earned a doctorate in education.

In addition to teaching and speaking to groups, Dr. Bodner has also worked individually with a wide variety of people, helping them plan their careers and increase their job satisfaction. She lives and works in the Kansas City, Missouri, metropolitan area.

VENDA RAYE-JOHNSON, M.A., L.P.C., N.C.C.C., is both a licensed professional counselor and a nationally certified career counselor in private practice. She has written numerous articles on career management and is the author of *Effective Networking*. In addition to her counseling and writing, she is an adjunct instructor at several colleges in Kansas City, and is a speaker and workshop presenter on topics pertaining to interpersonal communications and career management. She was named an Outstanding Young Woman in America in 1987.